*Also by John F. Gordon*

THE STAFFORDSHIRE BULL TERRIER OWNER'S ENCYCLOPAEDIA

THE SPANIEL OWNER'S ENCYCLOPAEDIA

ALL ABOUT THE COCKER SPANIEL

ALL ABOUT THE STAFFORDSHIRE BULL TERRIER

# All about the Boxer

JOHN F. GORDON

PELHAM BOOKS

PELHAM BOOKS

Published by the Penguin Group
27 Wrights Lane, London W8 5TZ, England
Viking Penguin Inc., 40 West 23rd Street, New York, New York 10010, USA
Penguin Books Australia Ltd, Ringwood, Victoria, Australia
Penguin Books Canada Ltd, 2801 John Street, Markham, Ontario, Canada L3R 1B4
Penguin Books (NZ) Ltd, 182–190 Wairau Road, Auckland 10, New Zealand

Penguin Books Ltd. Registered Offices: Harmondsworth, Middlesex, England

First published 1970

SECOND IMPRESSION 1976
REVISED EDITION 1978
REPRINTED 1987, 1988

ISBN 0 7207 1087 1 REVISED EDITION

(0 7207 0317 4 1ST EDITION)

*Printed in Great Britain by
BAS Printers Limited,
Over Wallop, Hampshire*

# Contents

# Illustrations

ACKNOWLEDGEMENTS

The photographs are by Diane Pearce, except 1 from the author's collection; 2 and 3 by Gerald Massey Esq.; 4 and 6 by Historic Dog Features; 7 by Mrs M. Knight; 9 by B.M.C.; 10 and 14 by Whimpanny; 11 by Foyle; 13 by Hartley; 16 by Mrs P. Heath; 17 by Crompton.

# Preface

The Boxer cult has spread in the last thirty years to every civilised land; a few individuals have known life in barbarous parts of the globe too, but wherever the Boxer has lived, his great adaptability, in-bred from his early days in rough sports, has made him a useful dog to have around. By being thus he has endeared himself to countless owners of every nationality and there persists still in full measure, a desire to learn more of the breed.

The Boxer is an old love of mine. Always a keen admirer of the Bull Breeds family and having owned many of its members, I confess a fascination for its history and gladiatorial background. When one prepares a monograph on a breed such as this, it is inevitably with a sense of having trodden somewhere along the line on ground which has already been adequately covered by earlier writers on the breed. This applies especially to matters of its history. However, most authors – and I am no exception – console themselves with the knowledge that their style and approach to the subject is distinct and much of the monograph will give the reader new material and offer him fresh food for thought on his chosen breed.

I have tried to make this work as complete as the space at my disposal permits. The main thing when writing about a breed is to put before its devotees essential facts of its origin and development in an interesting way and to discuss the breed's procreation, upbringing and exhibiting – all semi-technical matters, tried, tested and found good – in an easily understandable form. I hope I have achieved this to the reader's satisfaction.

John F. Gordon
Romford

## Preface to Revised Editions

I am pleased to note that a further revised edition of this book is required to meet the demand for Boxer literature. Necessary alterations to the text such as amendments to fees, health data etc. and the addition of a few new photographs will bring it up to date.

J.F.G.
1987

# 1 Origin and History

## Ancient forebears

As with all modern breeds of dog, it is virtually impossible to be specific in the complex matters of origin and ancestry. The Boxer is no exception to this difficulty, although we are aware that he stems firmly from a rootstock steeped in antiquity which he shares with the Old English Bulldog. Unlike that classic breed however, his more recent evolutionary progress, namely that which occurred during the last decades of the nineteenth century, remains clouded. This is probably due to the lack of data forthcoming from his Continental background and because of this we are left in doubt as to the formula employed in producing the much admired Boxer make and shape. This now accepted breed outline and type, especially the headpiece, is unique in dogdom; nevertheless, no one can be quite certain how it was devised.

With what factual material we are fortunate enough to possess, collected from the archives of the breed, it would seem that the early progenitors of the Boxer existed and ran as heavy dogs of the chase some six centuries and more before the birth of Christianity. The major ancestral type was clearly the Old Mastiff. This noble beast, much larger and more ferocious than any Mastiff we meet but occasionally today, was used for a variety of hunting sports, sometimes even as an aid in battle. This dog is described by Jesse in his *Anecdotes of Dogs*, 1858 as 'a dog of gigantic size, of a yellowish colour, with a black muzzle'. That he was bred extensively and shipped out to Rome and beyond by the Procurator Cynegii, appointed by Roman Emperors to supplement the fodder of the amphitheatres, we know. We are uncertain however, whether the dog of donkey-like proportions he was to encounter, do battle with and often vanquish in the arenas of Athens, descended from the Mastiff or indeed foreran him. This dog was known to the ancients as the Molossian, so named because he was bred and developed for gladiatorial sports at which he excelled, in the town of Molossi, situated in Epirus, a canton in the north-west of Ancient Greece. There is a plaster reproduction of such an animal in the Metropolitan Museum of Arts, New York. It is captioned The Molossian Dog of Athens, for to Athens many of these great creatures were despatched from the big breeding stables in the north to be used in the amphitheatre for fighting wild beasts and armed men. As their success and tremendous prowess at these 'sports' became recognised and admired, selected specimens were shipped out to other countries in the ancient world and bred there. In the transitory process and due to interbreeding with dogs indigenous to these lands, very often the progeny developed slight alteration in appearance from the parental stock. This variation in appearance would be often confined to coat texture and length, sometimes to head and muzzle, but seldom did it seem to affect the bulk and temperament of the original breed. As the Molossian became domiciled in different lands it was bred too freely by the countrymen, always with the sports of the arena in mind. The Molossian is depicted in *Icones Animalium*, 1780 by G. F. Riedel. The illustration is to be seen in the British Museum and those who look at it cannot help but see a dog whose points are much in common with the Mastiff. Therefore, we cannot ignore the assumption that the Molossian is probably the rightful ancestor of the Mastiff and that latter breed set its mark on the several types of Bulldog (or Bullenbeissers, as they were known on the Continent for many years) to produce in the end our handsome Boxer.

The great antiquity of the Mastiff, and the Molossian, can better be realised when one examines the ancient Egyptian, Greek and Roman friezes, depicting scenes of the hunt, where Mastiff-type dogs can be seen in violent action. Witness too the wonderful artistry of some Assyrian bas-relief work from the first millennium B.C. The finest art of this kind comes, we believe, from the period of the reign of Ashurbanipal, a sporting king who ruled over this ancient Semitic civilisation in North Mesopotamia, 668–633 B.C. The dogs shown in these hunts look very fast, in spite of their obvious bulk. Their ferocity was such that they were capable of pulling down, even killing the lion. They were of the Old Mastiff family clearly enough and prehistoric fossils which have been discovered indicate even more than pictures will, the great size and girth of the dog which preceded the European Mastiff, the Boxer's ancestor.

It is likely that such big dogs were brought from the Mediterranean lands to England by the itinerant trading Phoenicians long before the birth of Christ. Here they could have become domiciled and while not necessarily finding themselves involved in barbarous sports, would almost surely have been employed by our forefathers in helping to repel coastal invaders. In this way they became war dogs and notorious to many an uninvited guest to the shores. They must have greeted the Romans when they landed in England some two thousand years ago, for the poet Gratius Faliscus in A.D. 8 (published 1534) referred to them as the 'Pugnaces of Britain'. Later, Claudian described them as the 'broad-mouthed dogs' of Britain. It is feasible that the Britons cherished these dogs, certainly we learn that in due course, laws were made to protect them and one would assume that careful breeding would have produced by selection, even larger and more powerful animals, for size, strength, courage and tenacity were desiderata for the Mastiff type dog in those days. From the fragments of history available on the subject, we learn that many of these fine dogs were taken back to Italy to fight in the arena games, even against dogs already resident in Ancient Rome. The fact that when the British dogs arrived they were bigger and even fiercer than these speaks well for the breeders of Ancient Britain! In effect, these old dogs made their mark in Rome and their fame spread across the world. It is not surprising that their breeding influence extended too. Many modern breeds, some of them perhaps almost extinct today, owe their formation to these fighting Mastiffs of Britain. Breeds such as the Branchiero of Sicily, the Rottweiler of Southern Germany, the Tibetan Mastiff, the Dogue de Bordeaux of France, the English Bulldog and even the St Bernard owes to the Molossian ancestral affinity. More in line however, towards making the Boxer we know today was the Bullenbeisser. This 'breed's' influence extended across the whole of Europe, from France through Germany into Poland. Some say that it was closely related to the Dogue de Bordeaux and to compare these two old types from pictures there can be little doubt that this is true. To see how closely the Dogue de Bordeaux contributed towards the Boxer, look at the illustration of the antique bronze shown here. This is from the author's collection. It depicts a Dogue de Bordeaux or Bullenbeisser, seemingly escaped from its post and trailing a broken chain. It is trying to divest itself of a muzzle. This bronze, after C. H. Valton, *c*.1865 shows the type of over a century ago. No one can deny that a lot of the modern Boxer has been inherited from such a dog and it would seem unnecessary to seek much further for Boxer ancestry than the Bullen-beisser.

Bronze model of an early Boxer type, about a hundred years old.

THE BULLENBEISSER

This dog was popular, mainly in Germany for several centuries, where it was used for the 'ruder' hunting sports, such as at the larger wild animals of the day. At such hunts, much blood was spilt, considerable violence employed and there was a deal of mortality in dogs and horses as well as the hunted! The name Bullenbeisser means 'Bull-biter'; sometimes the name Bärenbeisser or 'Bearbiter' was used to name the dog. We assume the name depended largely on the use to which the dog was put by the people who owned him, but Bullenbeisser was the name most used. In medieval times, the breed was used to hunt the Aurochs or wild ox. This creature was probably hunted out of existence for it disappeared towards the end of the twelfth century on the Continent, a fate nearly suffered by its cousin the American bison. The German and French feudal lords of the day kept very large packs of dogs for hunting, in much the same way as the English kept Foxhounds. These fierce, fast dogs were maintained ready for the 'off' at a moment's notice through rough and rugged, often mountainous terrain. They would hunt anything they were called upon to, and the more savage the foe, the greater they indulged their own ferocity. That type of hunt was one of no quarter given, none expected and although the Bullenbeisser was often garbed in chainmail and padded sackcloth to protect his body and flanks from the lethal tusks, teeth and claws of maddened quarry, he was frequently killed. Production of the breed was given a fairly free hand by the overlords in view of the considerable losses experienced, but as breeding was almost entirely within the pack itself, type and style of the Bullenbeisser by in-breeding, suffered no adulteration. Thus, the breed maintained a type desirable for its task for many centuries.

Bärenbeisser attacking a bear (School of Samuel Howitt, 1765–1822).

The Bullenbeisser had a most intimidating aspect with his great biting head, the underhung jaw and split lip. Nevertheless, pictures and models from the past bear at least some resemblance to the modern Boxer, although the older breed was far bigger, cloddier and coarser than we claim to admire in modern times. His tail too would either have been left at its natural length or more often docked half way. Such matters as concern modern breeders, fine noble heads, hindquarter angulation and similar elegancies held no value with the old breeders. They looked for, nay, demanded speed, weight, and a big heartful of courage to do the job. The refinements of the show ring were matters which later architects of the breed have dealt with.

As the larger beasts of the forest and plain drifted painfully into extinction, due mainly to the predacity of Man, lesser animals such as the boar remained to give scant sport to the huntsman and his pack. It was not long before the big packs on the old Ducal estates became decimated, later to be dispersed almost entirely. The Bullenbeisser, poor fellow, drifted into a new sphere of existence, this one less noble, certainly less admired and respected, although let it be said that he was eminently suited to it. He became a 'Butcher's Dog' and as such he had to participate in the odious pastime of baiting the bull.

BULL BAITING

This is an ancient sport and it is believed to have existed on the Continent before being introduced into Britain with the Norman Conquest. Not only the bull, but all sorts of big, strong animals, usually tethered to a post or tree, were subjected to this sadistic pastime, big dogs of Mastiff proportions being usually employed. Animals such as the bear, lion, even the horse were not overlooked by promoters of the game, but they proved either too ponderous or lacking verve to make the pace fast and exciting. The bull, on the other hand, put up a pleasurable day's event. Powerful, yet fast and lusty, he always fought well and with great vigour. With his horns he could put paid to a few intruders and one slipped sharply under the dog's belly could throw the animal high into the air. Most of these dogs were owned by butchers, who promoted the sport and unless the unfortunate dog's owner could rush forward and catch the animal in his outstretched apron or slip a long pole beneath it as it fell and allow it to slide to the ground, to break its fall, it was seldom the dog took another run at the bull. Enthusiasts of the sport held the opinion that a baited bull's flesh was tenderer than the meat from an unbaited animal. The great torment to which the bull was put caused the blood to course freely and fast through its veins. Later, when the butchers killed the bull and roasted it, portions from the carcase were in great demand and sold at high prices. It is little wonder that the pastime took the fancy of the Continental public, just as it did in England and persisted for many years. In every town, and hamlet green, bull stakes were set up and on feast days especially, it was usual to bait a bull with ferocious dogs. The scenes at such events were often awful; it was not unusual for a bull in its agony, to break loose and rush through the town, knocking down and killing folk, causing others to be trampled upon and maiming the dogs which had been set upon him. At the end, he too would meet an awful end, clubbed or scythed brutally to death. Such scenes defy description. Some refer to them as the 'bad old days'. No doubt they were sad and brutish days for animals; their lot is better today for sure. One can hardly excuse such goings-on, but there was little else to do for amusement and the Continent and England too was cruel and rough-and-ready in its sports. In England, Royal patronage was given to the sport in the latter half of the sixteenth century and the aristocracy followed the participants, bull, bear and dog by name and career in much the same way as today football and cricket fans support their favourites! By this era, the pastime, although common enough in Germany, had not 'arrived' in the same spectacular way as it had in England. Nevertheless, the Continentals kept a close eye on English progress in the sport and were not slow in emulating any improvements in the game.

The dog was expected to bait the bull by pinning the larger animal to the ground by its nose and not lose its grip. Both dog and bull got very cunning at the game, the dog at getting a hold on the bull and the bull at avoiding the dog's jaws. The clever bull, anticipating a dog's rush, would paw the ground with a forefoot, scraping out a hole into which he would sink his nose out of the dog's reach. The dog, for his part, anxious to avoid a sharp horn in his side, or a toss in the air would often crawl along the ground to the bull on his belly. Usually, the bull was tethered so that he could operate only in a confined space of thirty feet diameter. The average Bullenbeisser in use for centuries, right up to the beginning of the nineteenth century was still a bulky animal; one could liken him almost to a small Mastiff. To some extent, although active for his size, he did little to contribute to a fast moving sport, which is what the sporting populace yearned for in their enthusiasm for the game. Consequently, a smaller, more agile Bulldog was evolved. How this was done we cannot be sure, but we know from experience with some of our modern breeds, the Poodle, the Schnauzer and the Bull Terrier in particular, that smaller forms have been evolved. In the three breeds referred to, these have resulted in Miniatures being produced. No Miniatures were wanted in the Bullenbeisser family, of that we can be certain, for such as these would have been useless to the sport; but animals which turned up smaller than normal in breeding programmes would have been conserved, possibly for domestic guard work. These specimens now came into their own and were used for breeding, producing a smaller form of Bullenbeisser and it is with this form of the breed that we are most concerned when we seek the immediate forerunner of the Boxer. The modern development of our Boxer will be discussed in later pages.

## Other progenitors

It was not until the beginning of the fifteenth century that much interest was shown in dogs by writers. In England, interesting material in the rare manuscript, *The Master of Game*, 1406–1413, is written on the Mastiff Group by Edward, Second Duke of York. Here, reference is made to the Alaunt, described as a short-headed dog, courageous and able to hang on to his quarry or adversary. This breed has been elsewhere reported as the Alan or Alano, which of course became the Spanish Bulldog, another variety closely akin to the Dogue de Bordeaux. Chaucer too in his *Knight's Tale*, describes Alaunts belonging to the King of Thrace:

'Aboute his char ther wenten whyte alaunts,
Twenty and mo, as grete as any steer,
To hunten at the leoun or the deer,
And folwed him, with mosel faste y-bounde,
Coleres of gold, and torets fyléd rounde.'

An interesting point is the mention here of colour – white. Present-day Mastiffs are invariably self-coloured, fawn or brindle. Old pictures of the Alaunt, an important member of the Mastiff family, show him in a variety of coat colours, often well patched or emblazoned with white, or even totally white, commoner to the modern Bulldog family than to Mastiffs. Alaunts were divided into classes – the Alaunts Gentil being used for domestic duties, guards and housedogs – or bandogs, as the English termed them. The Alaunts Ventreres were the hunting kind; these would have been the big ones, no doubt. Alaunts du Botcherie would have been the sort used in Bull-baiting, a smaller variety, lacking nothing however in strength and spring. On the famous Bayeux Tapestry, it is the Alaunts Ventreres that are pictured in embroidered work as long ago as nine hundred years. The Alaunts have long since fused their line into that of the Bullenbeisser and similar German varieties. They remain only in name to stir the imagination of canine historians.

The Bandogge or Bond-dog, whichever name you prefer, was really a forerunner of the Old English Bulldog or the Englische Dogge as he was know abroad. This Bandogge was an animal used for domestic guard duties, chained up most of the day, as his name implies, but let off occasionally to indulge for his master a morning's sport of bull-baiting. No proper division of the breeds (as we know them) was ever contemplated until 1570 when the Elizabethan sage Dr Johannes Caius detailed them in Latin in his *De Canibus Britannicis*. Some years later this was translated in to English by Abraham Fleming, and we read his description of the Mastyve or Bandogge '. . . vast, huge, stubborne, augly, and eager, of a heavy and burthenous body, and therefore of little swiftness, terrible and frightful to beholde, and more fearse and fell than any Arcadian curre'. The name Mastyve covered a multitude of canine types. Almost any huge dog or big-headed guard dog fell into the category. It has been suggested by writers that the name was a corruption of the old English word 'masty', meaning 'fat'. This is feasible for in the sixteenth century, at least, dogs were named according to either their function or appearance. Fleming shows us that Caius grouped his dogs in this way, referring to breeds other than Terriers, Hounds, Spaniels and Toys as *Canes Rustici* (dogs of the country). See Caius' table, top page 17.

The Bandogge existed in Britain and his counterpart abroad for many generations. He was a dog of Mastiff-cum-Bulldog form, although often enough any large guard dog of similar type and disposition would have been crossed with him. Apart from being feared for his vicious appearance and staunch devotion to guard work, he received scant respect from the public. In fact, he was regarded as a brainless monster by many. Even F. Cuvier was purported to have asserted that the Bulldog, who descended from the Bandogge, had a brain smaller in proportion than any other of his cogeners!* Such a statement is considered today so wide of the truth as to be laughable; stubborn the breed might well be, but never short of brains. Neither is there any reason to suppose that he varied from other canines four hundred years ago. A number of these early Bulldogs found their way to Germany and to divers places throughout Europe. In Germany they became known as the Englische Doggen and being of a more refined kind than the resident Bullenbeisser of the day, they speedily became fashionable. Both breeds, the German and the English were used together; this being inevitable and from the union there appeared a type which could perhaps be best described as smarter, more personable. From what eventually became a pure stock the seed of the modern Boxer was struck, in spite of the fact that undoubtedly both his parental types would have been maintained individually by their devotees. Strongly introduced from the Bullenbeisser side of the 'family' was the Brabanter. He is reported as being rather smaller in size than the kind encountered in the north of Germany. The artist Ridinger portrays him from the eighteenth century scene as a powerful, deep-through and well-coupled fawn coated dog with dark mask. In his native Brabant he too would have been used for various blood sports, although he was known too as a water-drawer, harnessed in quite tractable fashion to a small cart. Such inborn ability to perform well two such widely differing occupations speaks volumes for the breed's intelligence, and temperament. The modern Boxer has inherited such characteristics, making him what is probably the best all-purpose dog today.

*The Dog, In Health and Disease*, 1859 by 'Stonehenge' (J. H. Walsh).

| Dogges com-prehended in ye fourth secion are these | The Shep-herds Dogge The Mas-tive or Bandogge | which hath sundry names derived from sun-dry cir-cumstances as | The Keeper or Watchman The Butcher's Dogge The Messinger or Carrier The Mooner The Water Drawer The Tinckers Curr The Fencer |
|---|---|---|---|

## The nineteenth century

The German progenitor of the Boxer, like his English cousin the Bulldog, suffered a hard-living background to his life during this century. It was a legacy from his gladiatorial past, which was to require a difficult process of shedding if he was to endear himself to the world outside. His great attributes which included courage, tenacity, loyalty and fearlessness, meant little to the man in the street. These were things the bull and bear baiter looked for in his dog; even *he* did not admire them as characteristics, only as wager winners when he put his intrepid dog against its foe. The English dog was a shade luckier however, for in 1835 the Humane Act, inspired by the body we know now as the R.S.P.C.A. abolished the baiting of bulls in public. Up to this time the Bulldog and the ruffian, always at the dog's expense, had earned a disreputable living together. Royal accolade had been withdrawn from the sport long since and for some years the Bulldog's life had been unsavoury, to say the least. Now, with the 1835 Act he entered a new life, Admittedly, bull-baiting went on still, but these were more in the nature of hole-in-the-corner events, which lacked prestige and had scant impact on the community. The German Bulldog, already shaping up to become immediate progenitor to the Boxer was less fortunate. Still a despised breed, he had to wait amost another half century before his usefulness as a contributor to Boxer history was acknowledged.

At this stage, we are obliged to consider two theories of Boxer evolution. They are:

1. That the Boxer is actually a direct descendant of the original Bullenbeisser which lived prior to 1800, bred on more refined lines with no or very few English crossings.
2. That the Boxer's principal ancestors were the Bullenbeisser of medieval Europe and an English Bulldog of similar era.

We are obliged to give some support to the first story when we examine the old pictorial studies of the Bullenbeisser. We see a dog, certainly thick all through and cloddier than we want in the Boxer, but with an outline and with body properties which we know, as dog breeders, could have been fashioned into modern Boxer type by selective breeding. We can see in this ancient breed – the Bullenbeisser, characteristics of the skull, jaw-line, shoulders and topline which have been bequeathed to the modern Boxer. Head features need not worry us too much. Most modern breeds have heads which have been moulded fancier-fashion in recent years, these are faddist appurtenances, important today, but not so vital to the old breeders of the period. The theory is one which appeals to the breed enthusiast for it suggests that the Boxer descends from purer blood lines. However, we cannot dismiss the data from the past. This has come to us by the written word and from information passed by word of mouth from generations of breeders into the present century. This makes it reasonably certain that English Bulldog blood *was* mixed with that of the indigenous Bullenbeisser to produce in part, at least, a refined form of German Bulldog, later to be fashioned into the Boxer. The newcomer appeared in all the variety of colours we attribute to the Bulldog, fallows, fawns, chestnuts, brindles and even all whites. Certainly all the self colours with a few splashes and blazes of white were common, indicative of English Bulldog influence.

'Tyger and his Master': an early-nineteenth-century engraving.

Any dog breeder who knows his subject is aware that by careful selection and studious breeding over a comparatively short period, one can produce almost any desired shape, colour, type, size or variety of dog. To complete a proper picture, one should also breed for a desired temperament. To maintain the temperament of any breed is not very easy. Most varieties were bred and developed for a specific purpose. The old Bullenbeisser and the Bulldog were bred for blood sports. The fact that the baiting of the bull was a pastime rife in their time made it easy enough for the breeders to conserve and perpetuate the required temperament. Our modern Boxer was produced largely with beauty in mind, but he needs a proper breed temperament nevertheless. To be truthful, we want him to inherit the temperament of his forefathers. This is not an easy wish to realise for we cannot introduce our modern dog to a bull-baiting session on Sundays and Bank Holidays, for this is against the law. Dog-fighting once so very popular, now justly with a veil drawn over it as a degrading sport, might have kept Boxer spirit and fire at a high order. The fact of the matter is, that today, we have no true test of courage for our dog. We can never be quite sure that the dog we breed to our bitch carries the right sort of bold heart in his body. In the old days, they cared little for make and shape, as we have said. It was temperament that mattered most. Successful bull-baiting dog was bred to bitches proven thrice and more in the affray and no doubt about it, such dams threw the right sort of stock for which the old-time sportsman-breeder got good financial return in his day. The best we can do in modern times is to be cautious; make sure the dog we use is at least a good upstanding stallion at least in character and courage. Ensure too that the dam who has produced the puppy you buy is no shirker when it comes to action. Being selective in such matters is your contribution to Boxer future.

Let us accept then the Boxer is the scion of the Bullenbeisser and the more refined English Bulldog of the time. This is a factual breeding formula, aided by prudent selection and development. One might wonder how the unique Boxer head was fashioned, how such perfection in angulation was applied to the hindquarters especially. All these factors are discussed elsewhere in the book, but clearly they appeared, doubtless in moderate form now and again during early breeding. They were noted, admired and commended to the expert breeder as he progressed. This enthusiast would sort the wheat from the chaff in every litter. The old German breeders especially were disciplinarians in this. They wanted only the *best* from their stock and they would run on every puppy until it was assessable, keep the promising ones and dispose of the remainder, goodness knows where, but certainly where their effect on later development would be nullified. As the Boxer population increased and variations of type, as well as mutations were seen, outstanding physical (and mental) features were eagerly seized upon and developed and injected into later breeding programmes. This is how breed type was built and eventually spokeshaved to even better form. It is the way the Boxer was founded and shaped, the work being done with typical Teutonic thoroughness, for the Boxer today is a living example of the pedigree dog breeder's skill.

## Modern development

Emancipation for the Boxer did not commence much before the end of the nineteenth century. Even as late as 1880 records show signs of casual breeding between diverse types in Germany. This did little to contribute style and refinement to Boxer shape, for low-to-ground and cloddy types were rife.

In Britain, the picture was different. Dog-breeding was beginning to come into its own. The English Kennel Club had drawn up its first line of recognised breeds in 1874, some forty, in fact, classified by Rawdon B. Lee. This put them well in advance of the Germans whose interest in the subject had not developed such enthusiasm. Nevertheless, a lot of Germans were beginning to realise that *their* 'Bulldog' was a worthy breed and they commenced to view with some envy the progress with dogs in England, and decided to campaign their own dog into a 'true' breed. Little did they know at that time just how sensationally would the new breed 'catch on', or indeed how it would improve and assume regal pedigree excellence.

The earliest records show that in 1887 George Alt of Munich bought in France a bridle bitch which he named 'Alt's Flora'. She was mated to an unnamed Boxer from the locality, getting among other nice puppies G. Mühlbauer's 'Alt's Schecken', a parti-coloured bitch, who in turn was mated to 'Tom', the famous (by virtue of his role in early Boxer breeding) white English Bulldog. This dog, owned by Dr Tönniessen of Munich would have been nothing like the Bulldog we know today, he did in fact look much more like a Boxer! Tom's part in this brief saga may well have proved useful in laying a foundation for strong heads in the breed, although some people seem to blame him for the sudden appearance of all-white coats in the strain. Without doubt he may have contributed to the matter, but in this period a lot of indiscriminate mating was going on, using imported stock from England. Almost anything in the 'Bull' category – Bulldogs, Bull Terriers, were used to Boxer bitches and little was done to rectify this sad state of affairs until the breed began to appear at dog shows, upon which the matter was taken in hand more conscientiously.

The first Boxer to be registered in the original German Boxer Stud Book was 'Flocki' sired by 'Tom' out of 'Alt's Schecken'. This dog then was half English Bulldog, he was a brindle and born 26 February 1895, bred by Mr A. Nerf. Shown at Munich show in 1895 he was the only entry. The German Boxer Club was formed one year later and from that point interest in the breed soared to a high level. However, there remained a lot of 'cleaning-up' to do, not only of the alien blood which existed in some of the dogs, but among the members of the Club, where dissent was rife. Some members, fortunately they were in the minority, favoured the Old English Bulldog type, whereas the rest aimed to disperse foreign characteristics. Eventually, the arguments were eliminated and the Club settled down to studying the Boxer and improving it, this being the prime function of any dog club or society. This occurred in 1910, by which time a number of smaller clubs had sprung up in Germany and the Netherlands. The official Boxer Stud Book was published in 1904 and the same year saw the appearance of *Boxer Blätter* at the hand of Dr Neumann. This magazine has proved a source of great interest and education to Boxer lovers, especially when information on early dogs has been wanted. It is said that there is no present-day Boxer whose pedigree does not trace right back to the Munich Boxers; records fortunately, are such that this can be proven to those who seek traditional glory in their dogs. The original Standard of the Breed was for many years a bone of contention among German fanciers. It had a stormy passage at many meetings until it was accepted finally in 1905. Once adopted, the breed was given a clear path of progress for its breeding programme and since then that advance has been steady, broken only in the first quarter of this century by World War I. Even in those bad years, the Boxer distinguished himself as a competent war dog and served well his countries. In spite of all this, the Boxer did not take a proper foothold in Germany until nearly ten years after the Armistice by which time he was being used quite extensively by the Police. Shortly following this the British showed an interest in him and he has developed well here, almost to 'boom' proportions. America took him to her bosom almost a decade later; there he is a leader in the popularity stakes and it would not seem too optimistic to assume that there is still a great potential to be realised.

## Early imports

It was as early as 1919 when Dr McMaster is reported to have purchased a dog and bitch from Germany and brought them to his home in Ballymena, Northern Ireland, but the first Boxer to be imported to England was 'Gretl von der Boxerstadt' (No. 1693/37) who arrived in whelp to 'Hansel von Biederstein'. Mrs C. Sprigge supervised the importation and whelping in quarantine and from the litter came the first British Boxer Ch. 'Horsa of Leith Hill', owned by Mrs. H. Caro.

Virtually at the same time Mr Allon Dawson started importing and to the world famous 'Stainburndorf' Boxer kennels can go most of the credit for putting the breed 'on the map' in Britain. He was shortly joined by many other enthusiasts, some of whom are alive today. To mention their names is too great a task, but the famous names of their kennels will echo the history of this advancing breed. By commencement of World War II, the Boxer was becoming well established in Britain. He was in constant attendance at all the important shows and the people who proudly owned him ensured that he was well publicised. Of course, breeding had to be cut almost to nothing during the war, although a few diehards managed to produce the odd litter or two. With the end of hostilities, the Boxer, like other breeds, was in a sad way numerically and to some his type had suffered due to restricted and casual breeding. A number of post-war enthusiasts together with a few of the original breeders introduced fresh blood from the Continent. With some of the imports they brought in troubles too, most of these being physical point deficiencies. This was to be expected of course, and had to be dealt with. One of the worst worries centred around ears. Britain will not countenance earcropping its dogs, neither will it encourage the system by allowing cropped-ear dogs to be exhibited for competition. In countries such as Germany and America where no such rule exists, the breeders may not care how big and untidy the ears grow on their Boxers, for they know that when the animal is old enough these appendages can be trimmed down to smart shape and size. In fact, big ears are better to trim than small ones; they allow more scope for the cropper. It can be seen then just how important it was for British breeders especially to *breed* a small neat ear. The old Bull Terrier people had the same problem here before 1900 and they dealt with the matter the hard way – by careful selection over a period, breeding only to the dogs with the neatest erect ears. To judge how successful they were you need only look at the Bull Terrier ring at any championship show. Similar skill was extended to the Boxer as a whole and within five years after the war an excellent standard had been achieved, not very far behind the high overall quality already achieved by the Germans. The German system of breeding is a highly organised one, needing considerable discipline on the part of the breeders, but properly applied it has shown outstanding results.

## German Boxer Club Breeding System

Almost from the inception of scientific Boxer breeding in Germany, the subject has been viewed and dealt with very seriously. The German Boxer Club has made rigid rules on the methods of breeding to be followed and a member is obliged to follow them slavishly, otherwise his bitch's progeny will never be allowed entry registration in the official Stud Book.

The key to the German system is to select a few outstanding stud dogs, proven by the quality of their get. Every bitch, as she comes ready for mating is relegated to one of these sires and her owner has no say in the matter, apart from perhaps a choice from the given names of three studs. The bitch herself is required to be at least twenty months old before she can be mated and to have received a medium grade qualifying award at a recognised show. She must also have satisfied a test for guard-dog ability, true breed temperament and character. The whole process is supervised by a Breed Warden who is trusted to attend to arrangements in a correct way. Should the bitch not qualify for a show award, by reason of her inability to attend such an event, then a delegation from the Club must see her and pass her as approved. The mating itself has to be witnessed by a Club member and a certificate signed confirming it.

When the litter arrives it has to be examined by the Chairman of the local Boxer Club. He has to attend the breeder's home within four days of the birth and go over each puppy for type and quality and soundness. Any number of puppies over six will have to be destroyed, for that is the Club rule. The Chairman will then dock the puppies' tails. Later, when the puppies are eight weeks of age, they will be inspected again for soundness and this being ensured with all other things in good order, the ears will be cropped. Certificates of application for Registration are then completed and after the Chairman has reported to his Club committee that every rule has been observed correctly, registration is thereupon granted.

To the British and American minds this process savours of dictatorship in dogdom. A lot of fanciers dislike the idea of the system and vow they would not contribute to it if it was employed in Britain. The Germans however, like the idea for they know it gets good results. The system is one of concentrated line-breeding, using expertly chosen stud dogs of the correct bloodlines and physical as well as temperamental perfections. It is quite certain that if this system is the foundation upon which Germans have developed their modern Boxer excellence, then it is a good system, whatever the critics have to say about it being autocratic and so on. To produce good quality articles in any business, one must have rules, rigid discipline and application to the job in hand. The Germans, natural exponents of such characteristics, have proved how quickly beautiful Boxers can be produced, even against the loss of time which handicapped their progress while the early German dog-owners remained scornful of scientific dog-breeding.

## The name?

A deal of mystery surrounds the name of Boxer. No one is quite sure where it came from, although a number of opinions have been proffered. It has been stated that the old, smaller kind of Bullenbeisser, the Brabanter was often referred to as a 'Boxl'. If this is true, then one has a fairly ready explanation, for 'Boxl' could easily have turned into 'Boxer'. Another writer tells us that an early contributor to the modern Boxer's bloodlines, was named 'Boxl' and the name sprang from his. Nothing is definite, no more is it that the name came from the Boxer's habit of using his paws in sparring fashion when at play or when countering another dog. Certainly, if you seek the word 'Boxer' in a German-English dictionary you will find it defined as 'boxer, pugilist, prize-fighter', but this means nothing really, for a boxer (pugilist) is a boxer in most of the world's modern languages wherever that sport is discussed. It is likely that the English, whose 'show' interest in the breed foreran that of the Germans, sought a 'good' name for it. Bullenbeisser would not have been a palatable word for the insular English tongue. A snappier, more descriptive name would be preferred. One might think that the name 'German Bulldog' would have suited, but at the time the breed was being introduced to England around the turn of the century, the very name 'German' connected with it would have ruined its chances of popularity. The name 'beisser' meaning 'biter', might well have sounded like 'boxer' to British ears when articulated in the Teutonic tongue and became corrupted thus. Even more likely, it is felt that a name was sought for a breed whose outstanding physical characteristic at the time was a flat-nosed, boxer-like, even plug-ugly face. Maybe it seemed appropriate then just to call it Boxer . . . ?

## Appearance in art and literature

The forebears of our modern Boxer have been quite freely depicted in art, J. E. Ridinger, the German painter and engraver, 1698–1767 being responsible for some wonderful, informative work on the Bullenbeisser, showing him in sport and repose. George Morland the English painter, 1763–1804 is of particular interest to us, for some of his dogs were Boxers, shown just as the breed was beginning to take shape and enter the nineteenth century. The engraving by James Linnell of Morland's 'The Turnpike Gate', published in 1806 shows what seems a particularly good specimen of the era. The same artists's 'The Country Butcher', engraved by J. R. Smith, published 1802 depicts a typical old time Boxer. Probably the subject himself was an early bull-baiter known as a 'Butcher's Dog' strongly favouring certain physical features in our modern breed.

'Jem Crow and Cartache': an engraving by W. R. Smith after Cole, showing an early Boxer type.

Gerald Massey the antiquarian offered for sale in 1945 two good and useful art examples of the Boxer. One, called 'Le Testament de la Tulipe' a black-and-white line engraving by Beauvarlet after Lenfant, published in Paris c.1770, showed a military scene with a large Boxer bitch, crop-eared. The other was 'Drinking Scene in a Tavern', engraving by Delius after Bohmer, published in Berlin, c.1840. Three dogs are shown, one an early type of Boxer, tan-coloured and crop-eared. The city of Munich is well endowed, as one might expect, with art which features old Boxer-type dogs. A visit to the National Museum there is well worth while; in fact, any enthusiast visiting Germany could do worse than to visit local museums where often likenesses of early Boxer-type dogs can be found.

In written work, so far as early writings are concerned, there is little to peruse. Many of the old dog writers could bring in the Boxer only by his progenitors. There is much to read of the Mastiff, the Bullenbeisser and the Bulldog. A good deal of this is bound up with divers kinds of bull-baiting and combat dogs, from which we are perforce able to sort out the types which are acceptable to us as forerunners of the Boxer. The student is advised to consider these early aspects of the Boxer in spite of the fact that type and outline today varies so much with the ancestral stock. In the study of breed evolution one needs to develop an eye for the unfolding of canine form from its early stages to its modern stock form. The expert may well be allowed to employ his imagination in the task, for without this no true picture of a breed's progress throughout the centuries could ever be formed.

# 2 The Standard

The Boxer Standard is intended solely as a guide to judges, breeders and breed lovers. It is worded so that the enthusiast can obtain in his 'mind's eye' a picture of the perfect Boxer. Theoretically, knowing then what the paragon of Boxers should look like, he should as a judge be able to set this standard of perfection against the exhibits before him and grade them accordingly. As a breeder he should be impartial enough to look at his own Boxer and realise immediately its deficiencies, aiming at once in his breeding campaign to correct these faults in the next litter! Of course, it is known that these things just do not happen, although many try to achieve perfection in their judging and breeding. At least, the official breed Standard is a useful, important, even essential document in Boxerdom. Without it, breeders would not have a target on which to set their sights. For this reason alone, every Boxer fancier should study it carefully so that he knows it thoroughly. As the chapter on Judging will show, it is necessary to interpret the Standard and apply this to the living flesh.

The Standard was evolved by experts in 1950 by Boxer clubs extant in Britain at that time. Its original form can be found in *Kennel Club Standards of the Breeds, Non-Sporting Breeds, Working Group*, Ref,Z(5). In 1986 a form of 'tidying-up' was prepared by The Kennel Club with the cooperation of breed clubs and this was presented in 1987. This document is more condensed and succinct and now comprises the current Boxer Standard. It is reproduced by kind permission of The Kennel Club and official copies are obtainable at the Club's London address (see Appendix 2) on payment of a nominal sum.

## The Boxer Standard

GENERAL APPEARANCE: Great nobility, smooth coated, medium sized, square build, strong bone and evident well developed muscles.

CHARACTERISTICS: Lively, strong, loyal to owner and family, but distrustful of strangers. Obedient, friendly at play, but with guarding instinct.

TEMPERAMENT: Equable, biddable, fearless, self-assured.

HEAD AND SKULL: Head imparts its unique individual stamp and is in proportion to body, appearing neither light nor too heavy. Skull lean without exaggerated cheek muscles. Muzzle broad, deep and powerful, never narrow, pointed, short or shallow. Balance of skull and muzzle essential, with muzzle never appearing small, viewed from any angle. Skull cleanly covered, showing no wrinkle, except when alerted. Creases present from root of nose running down sides of muzzle. Dark mask confined to muzzle,

distinctly contrasting with colour of head, even when white is present. Lower jaw undershot, curving slightly upward. Upper jaw broad where attached to skull, tapering very slightly to front. Muzzle shape completed by upper lips, thick and well padded, supported by well separated canine teeth of lower jaw. Lower edge of upper lip rests on edge of lower lip, so that chin is clearly perceptible when viewed from front or side. Lower jaw never to obscure front of upper lip, neither should teeth nor tongue be visible when mouth closed. Top of skull slightly arched, not rounded, nor too flat and broad. Occiput not too pronounced. Distinct stop, bridge of nose never forced back into forehead, nor should it be downfaced. Length of muzzle measured from tip of nose to inside corner of eye is one third length of head measured from tip of nose to occiput. Nose broad, black, slightly turned up, wide nostrils with well defined line between. Tip of nose set slightly higher than root of muzzle. Cheeks powerfully developed, never bulging.

Mr Ingram's Ch. Bockendon Buchanan.

Monsieur R. Triquet of Bruay's Ch. Orauch. A Dogue de Bordeaux associated with the very early Bullenbeiser bloodlines from which the Boxer sprang. Used in the Roman arenas.

EYES: Dark brown, forward looking, not too small, protruding or deeply set. Showing lively intelligent expression. Dark rims with good pigmentation showing no haw.

EARS: Moderate size, thin, set wide apart on highest part of skull lying flat and close to cheek in repose, but falling forward with definite crease when alert.

MOUTH: Undershot jaw, canines set wide apart with incisors (6) in straight line in lower jaw. In upper jaw set in line curving slightly forward. Bite powerful and sound, with teeth set in normal arrangement.

NECK: Round, of ample length, strong, muscular, clean cut, no dewlap. Distinctly marked nape and elegant arch down to withers.

FOREQUARTERS: Shoulders long and sloping, close lying, not excessively covered with muscle. Upper arm long, making right angle to shoulder blade. Forelegs seen from front, straight, parallel, with strong bone. Elbows not too close or standing too far from chest wall. Forearms perpendicular, long and firmly muscled. Pasterns short, clearly defined, but not distended, slightly slanted.

BODY: In profile square, length from forechest to rear of upper thigh equal to height at withers. Chest deep, reaching to elbows. Depth of chest half height at withers. Ribs well arched, not barrel shaped, extending well to

Mrs M. Knight's
Swanfield Sun Satyr.

Mrs W. Rahder's
Ch. Rahdavons
Remember Me.

rear. Withers clearly defined. Back short, straight, slightly sloping, broad and strongly muscled. Loin short, well tucked up and taut. Lower abdominal line blends into curve to rear.

HINDQUARTERS: Very strong with muscles hard and standing out noticeably under skin. Thighs broad and curved. Broad croup slightly sloped, with flat, broad arch. Pelvis long and broad. Upper and lower thigh long. Good hind angulation, when standing the stifle is directly under the hip protruberance. Seen from side, leg from hock joint to foot not quite vertical. Seen from behind, legs straight, hock joints clean, with powerful rear pads.

FEET: Front feet small and catlike, with well arched toes, and hard pads, hind feet slightly longer.

TAIL: Set on high, customarily docked and carried upward.

GAIT/MOVEMENT: Strong, powerful with noble bearing, reaching well forward, and with driving action of hindquarters. In profile stride free and ground covering.

COAT: Short, glossy, smooth and tight to body.

COLOUR: Fawn or brindle. White markings acceptable not exceeding one third of ground colour.

Fawn: Various shades from dark deer red to light fawn.

Brindle: Black stripes on previously described fawn shades, running parallel to ribs all over body. Stripes contrast distinctly to ground colour, neither too close not too thinly dispersed. Ground colour clear, not intermingling with stripes.

SIZE: Height: Dogs 57–63 cms. ($22\frac{1}{2}$–25 ins.); Bitches: 53–59 cms. (21–23 ins.). Weight: Dogs approximately 30–32 kg. (66–70 lbs.); Bitches approximately 25–27 kg. (55–60 lbs.).

FAULTS: Any departure from the foregoing points should be considered a fault and the seriousness with which the fault should be regarded should be in exact proportion to its degree.

Dr B. M. Cattanach's Ch. Steynmere Night Rider.

NOTE: Male animals should have two apparently normal testicles fully descended into the scrotum.

## The Standard interpreted

It can be stated categorically that the perfect Boxer does not exist. There are quite a number of very good specimens about, some of them show dogs and Champions to boot, but any Boxer who can rightly claim eighty per cent perfection is indeed a miraculous specimen! This means then that there is still a long way to go before total perfection is achieved. Every Boxer generation gets us nearer to the target perhaps – at least, that is what we hope and trust. To get top-flight Boxers one needs skill, knowledge and certainly a modicum of luck. At least, some of the knowledge required involves a clear understanding of the Standard and an ability to interpret it. One way to start self-tuition is to 'borrow' the best specimen you know and read the Standard *at* him – all the time savouring the component parts of the dog with the relevant sections of the written description. Start with the:

GENERAL APPEARANCE: Demeanour is important. His gait and carriage *has* to proclaim pedigree Boxer nobility. Consider this phrase carefully – if the

M. and J. Hambleton's Ch. Marbleton Dressed to Kill.

dog does not possess that quality, it will stand out just as surely as if he does. He should look pleasant, alert and keen, quite determined and self-provident. Expression is important; should it fail to conform to true Boxer outlook then there is something which causes this, so closer inspection must be made. It is probably because the eyes are either too small, too protuberant or displeasing in colour. Look at the musculation; the shape of the muscles should be long rather than bumpy. The latter sort are not much good for a free roomy stride which the Standard demands. A long muscle is a lasting one, ideal for a dog requiring stamina in action. Insist upon elegance and strength in the Boxer. Long musculation lends itself to elegance whereas bulky, bumpy muscles do not. What about Balance? Imagine a thread coming down from the sky and connecting with the dog at the point of centre of gravity, usually a point at mid-upper body right behind the shoulder. Imagine the thread raised by an invisible hand and the dog lifted off ground level. If he is balanced properly, neither end will go up or down. If his head is too big, disproportionate to his body, down

Ann M. Podmore's Ch. Dallgerry Golden Bracken.

Mr Thomas's Ch. Carzanlain Opus Too.

will go the head, up the tail end. If he is mean in head and fat over the loins, down will go the rear end, up the head. Both examples show an unbalanced dog. A good specimen must be balanced well from all angles. Another thing – do all the parts of the body fuse well from all angles? It is not generally realised that a Boxer can possess a wonderful head, an ideal front, a grand body, superior hindquarters, lovely legs and feet – and yet be a poor specimen! The reason may well be that all the parts mentioned do not *flow* into the shoulders, the shoulders seem apart from the body structure and the body in its turn seems to disown the legs, while the feet might just as well belong to another dog! It is all a matter of correct coupling and some dogs appear to lack proper integration. Such animals are basically unsound of course, and the degree of unsoundness is invariably revealed with the animal's movement. The gait will be quite untypical of the breed. A Boxer so ill-favoured is of no use to the discerning breeder and is best discarded.

THE HEAD: The Boxer headpiece is unique. As with most breeds it is of paramount importance. When value points were a feature of breed judging, the head always held more points value than other body features.

We do not want dogs which fail in any department, but one thing they must not fail in and that is head quality. Admittedly, the Boxer head is a rugged, handsome feature, but unlike some rugged characteristics it *must* be clean-cut, no matter from which angle it is viewed. When the head is examined – and it is recommended that a good deal of time is spent on this important section – it should be found that no matter from whichever angle you view it, the muzzle must appear always right in its proportion to the skull. The muzzle is a vital feature; if too narrow, too shallow, too long, too short – the effect of the true Boxer head is lost. The lips also contribute to the picture. The repandus (or bent upward underjaw) must never rise above the upper lip level, neither should there be any diminution of the chin, which should be wide. A dog lacking chin, lacks Boxer expression. It should never be possible to discern teeth and tongue when the mouth is closed. Stop is an essential feature of the overall head study. Lack of stop means poor muzzle and often contributes to a snipey, sometimes down-faced effect, which in this breed is completely undesirable. As with most breeds, a stud dog *must* have an ideal breed head if he is going to prove fashionable and attract keen breeders. Lastly, take a look in the mouth. Heed particularly a wry mouth; this being a formation where the upper incisors obliquely cross the lower

M. and J. Hambleton's Abgar v. Bernmariek of Marbleton. Imported Dutch Boxer.

M. and J.
Hambleton's Dolf
Buhe Farm of
Marbleton. Imported
Dutch Boxer.

ones. It is a bad fault as it makes for an ineffective bite, a bad feature in dogs of all breeds. Further, it is a serious transmittable fault in breeding and any stud dog so endowed may well prove a producer of embarrassing stock.

BODY: It has been explained already how the departments of the body can appear independent of the whole and how this detracts from correct movement and soundness. This understood, it is necessary to look at the topline. The line should be straight from shoulders to croup. Any undue 'roaching' or convex backline from the withers with particular emphasis over the loins shows a distinct weakness and it is a bad fault. Any dog so affected will lack stamina and move indeterminately. A backline which drops badly down where the tail is set on is a fault, a weakness, which is indicated immediately as soon as the dog moves away. Keep an eye on the bend of stifle too. This should be well bent, never straight. A straight stifle means that musculation of the thighs is inferior. A dog like the Boxer needs to propel himself forcibly. To do this he needs strongly muscled hindquarters, and straight stifles accompanied with light thigh muscu-lation militate at once against powerful propulsion. The hocks too should be quite low and directly under the dog's hind end, the lower part with the strong rear pads at a slight angle in from the point of hock.

FAULTS: It is of course important that the student acquaints himself with these, but assessment of a dog should be always in positive vein, i.e. look for the *good* points first and assess on good points. Faults are negative factors and must therefore take second place in any reckoning.

TYPE: Type is the quality essential to a dog if he is to approximate or represent the ideal model of a Boxer, based upon the Boxer breed Standard as drawn up by a body of recognised experts. A dog which has 'type' is one who though not necessarily perfect embodies much of the ideal – conversely, a dog 'lacking type' is one who though possibly possessing several good points is a long way from being a living model of the breed's ideal. In the sections 'General Appearance' and 'Body' under in-terpretation review above, it has been explained how a dog with excellent component parts, but without physical orientation to fuse these into a pleasing whole, *must* be unsound. On the other hand, it is feasible that an unsound dog could teem with type, for soundness is unaffected by type and vice versa. Type as such is not detailed in the Boxer breed Standard; nevertheless it is an essential feature of the Boxer, but it must exist with Soundness.

SOUNDNESS: It must be understood that soundness can be inherited or acquired. A dog, following an accident perhaps, is unsound. As long as he limps because his damaged leg hurts he remains unsound. His temporary unsoundness is not thrown off until the pain stops and he stops limping. This type of soundness concerns us little; for it will not be passed on to the animal's progeny, being non-genetic. Soundness, like Type, must be understood when interpreting the Standard, in spite of the fact that neither are mentioned. Anatomical unsoundness includes structural faults such as upright shoulders, which in a Boxer would produce stilted action and probably coarse formation of the neck and thorax. Cow-hocks, where the points of the hocks turn towards each other, are often caused by muscular weakness; the second thigh or hocks being too long; even a general structural weakness could be the reason. An exceptionally narrow pelvis would cause an exhibit to move too close together behind when going away. The dog's rear view is one entirely lacking muscular strength, the effect of angulation is absent and the fault is normally one of generic origin and being so, its effect can be lessened only by careful breeding. Loose elbows (out at elbows) is another generic fault and one certain to damn the chances of any prospective show or stud dog. This fault can be induced or acquired – either by the effect of rickets in puppyhood or bad lead training. A number of other physical unsoundnesses can occur in dogs; the more obvious ones being easily recognised. Unfortunately, some of them, such as acquired deafness and acquired as well as inherited eyesight failings, impotency, etc. are not. These faults are normally left to the honesty and integrity of the owners to admit them and it speaks highly for them that on the odd occasions when regressive conditions have appeared in Boxers, they have not been slow to reveal the facts for the benefit of their breed.

In effect, anything which impairs a Boxer's usefulness, whether this is permanent or temporary in its nature, is an unsoundness. It *can* apply to a Boxer who is below par in health and condition, working efficiency, action or character. Many things contribute to unsoundness – bad positioning while in foetal form in the dam, the effect of transient local pressure and obstructed circulation, even faulty pre-natal feeding of the dam. In puppyhood, unsoundness can be caused by faulty rearing, even too much or too little exercise or the aftermath of contracted disease. Breeders contemplating the use of an unsound dog should examine closely its history of unsoundness as well as its nature. It may well be that a dog with *acquired* features of unsoundness could prove a useful parent, whereas one with a genetic anatomical fault is quite useless in the breeding field.

EARS: In Britain where ear-cropping is taboo, breeders must watch carefully the size of the ears they produce in their puppies. In America and other countries where cropping is generally permitted, it does not matter so much for oversized ears can be trimmed down to shape, as required. Naturally, overseas breeders are fully conscious of this and endeavour to maintain ears of moderate size in the puppies they breed. However British Boxers and those of countries which frown on cropping have to produce ears which are modest in size, set nice and high on the skull and lying flat and close to the cheeks. Untidy ears take away points in the judge's final mark-up for general appearance and infringe the Standard's requirements.

COLOUR: The Standard permits fawns and brindles in their various shades from light to dark. Dilute fawns are unpleasant and so are indistinctly marked black brindles, with hardly any brindling; both are undesirable. All-white Boxers and those with more than one-third of their coat white are never exhibited. White markings are otherwise allowed and when white appears on the Boxer Muzzle its outline must show the essential dark mask.

Other aspects of the Boxer's general characteristics revealed in the show ring are discussed in a later Chapter – Judging the Boxer.

Mrs C. Wilson-
Wiley's Ch.
Wardrobes Flashing
Stream.

Mrs P. Heath's Ch.
Seefeld Picasso.

# 3 Breeding

Every lover of the Boxer should want to contribute to the breed's improvement. Breeding dogs is a most fascinating pastime and whether it is engaged upon as a business or a hobby, it can often prove rewarding. The production of pure-bred dogs conforming as near as possible to the current Boxer breed Standard should be the aim of the true fancier. Very few dog owners either understand or care much for genetics, certainly not many people can claim a knowledge of the subject. Those who do, learn one thing quickly – that it is virtually impossible to deduce a Boxer's breeding potential from his or her appearance alone. Equally impossible, one cannot assess potential from pedigree alone. The formula to work with is Appearance plus Pedigree, but even so, the breeder *must* know what he is looking for in the dog he examines and he *must* know how to read a pedigree. Dogs have faults (and as far as I am aware, the perfect one has not yet been bred); some of these being serious and transmittable, others of little consequence, the latter being easily disposable, the former requiring calculated attack to prevent their appearance in the progeny. This is where knowledgeable pedigree reading comes into use. To know each and every dog on the two pedigrees of a pair to be mated is invaluable. Unfortunately, it is not always possible to obtain such specialised knowledge of the ancestry shown in these documents, although often enough a good deal of worthwhile information can be gleaned from oldtimers in the breed whose memories can be persuaded to go back reliably down the show years. It is advisable to complete a sort of dossier on each dog and bitch, when not only their names but their bad as well as their good points will be revealed to the modern student. To the owner of the dog in the proposed mating pair it may become apparent at once from such data why his Boxer lacks good ear carriage, or to the bitch's owner why his female carries her stern a fraction too low. He will observe faults which appear in duplicate, even triplicate in the breeding. One hopes that if he observes again such faults in the male's pedigree that he would at once dismiss the ideas of bringing them together for he would then be adding further multiples of such faults to the breeding of their progeny. The foregoing example is perhaps sketchy, but no doubt it will serve to show the principle involved by studying Appearance and Pedigree when striving for good Boxers. It is most important when perfecting one's stock to observe keenly and practise carefully in breeding. When preparing a pedigree for study, one of at least five generations should be used. With the annotations you put against each name on that pedigree you will transform the dossier into something vital and revealing as to the breeding value of the animal studied. In effect, by examining the living Boxer you will ascertain the *visual* defects he possesses; by the study of pedigree you will discover the *hidden* faults he carries. The inter-related discoveries made must guide you when planning your breeding programme.

LINE BREEDING

This is probably the best method for cementing the quality of one's stock in breeding. The system is basically similar to that of close In-breeding but it takes rather longer to establish purity of strain. It does not entail so much culling of unwanted stock and for the average breeder it is much safer and more economical in the early establishment of his work. Line breeding includes the following crosses:

Grand-sire to grand-daughter
Grand-dam to grandson
Cousin to cousin

In this, one ancestor would appear twice in the previous three generations, but not within the last two. The term Line-breeding is often extended to include pedigrees in which one ancestor appears twice within the last five generations. A good deal of care has to be used when employing the method so that undesirable traits are prevented from rising to the surface and becoming fixed. When this occurs, there becomes atavism or reversion to early type.

Once a pure strain has been established by this method, not a lot can be done to improve it while the breeder continues to employ his own stock. At this stage it frequently becomes prudent to introduce new blood and here lies some danger. The dog to be used needs thorough 'vetting' as far as his effect in breeding is concerned. It is wiser to use a sire whose worth in the breeding field has already been clearly and irrefutably established than to employ a dog, perhaps better as a specimen or even in breeding – merely because of these attributes and economy. An untried youngster of such calibre might well ruin in no time the efforts of a breeder's lifetime. There is no difficulty in finding out what a stud dog has got in his career; show results tell most of the story and the people 'in the know' in the Boxer world are often the most successful exhibitors who can recount almost any stud dog's position in breed society, which is based on the quality and success of his get.

No two dogs are identical, even though they are of the same gene construction. I have no intention of getting on to the science of Genetics, for this is a specialised field which has its own books, apart from the fact that I believe most dog owners prefer not to apply themselves too closely to the subject, at least in the early stages of their enthusiasm for their breed. When slight variations in pure lines are noted, it can sometimes be attributed to environment. Such variations are therefore acquired or non-inherited as opposed to generic. To mention only a few such effects one can consider fluted bone, splayed feet, loose shoulders, cow-hocks, puny structure and similar weaknesses, all the results of poor environment, possibly ill-treatment. Such faults, as they are, are not necessarily prone to affect an animal's progeny, providing of course they were acquired during that animal's development. The ordinary process of selection need not be affected by them. On the other hand, dogs who show the effects of undesirable mutations must be disposed of immediately for they can contribute only harm to the strain. Undesirable features of any sort must be eradicated as soon as they are noted. The only stock to keep is that which can maintain the good standard of strain you have aimed for.

IN-BREEDING

This is strictly speaking the mating of relatives. It is not likely to achieve any success unless the Boxers involved are all of a high quality, physically and mentally. It is useless to try for success in this field with 'sports' (chance-bred good ones) or mediocre animals. Only top class material must be used in such breeding and by this is meant animals of high general quality and reasonably free from defects. If you try in-breeding with material which does not conform thus you are doomed to failure. When you enter into the field of in-breeding you expect to produce stock which does not vary, litter by litter. The longer the system is continued the greater the 'fix' becomes and this includes both good and bad points, where each exist. As each generation is planned the clever breeder weighs up his current parental material. From it he assesses the balance between good and bad points in his strain. He aims at once to maintain the good and breed out the bad by rigorously culling his stock. Over a period of generations of in-breeding he should be in a position to do this to his own satisfaction and for the purity of his strain. If he ignores or overlooks the defects he will do so to his own disadvantage for the longer defects are maintained the greater the effort which will be required to disperse them, if indeed this proves possible without the ruination of his strain.

In conclusion it should be remembered that any programme of in-breeding must be conducted with superior and sound stock of the finest standard quality. To enter the field with anything which savours of the mediocre is to court disaster.

OUT-CROSSING

Too many people are of the opinion that out-crossing, that is the introduction of new blood into an established strain, has the magical power of improving, invigorating even producing something sensational in that strain. This is a fallacy – not only is it impossible for an out-cross to eliminate a fault in a single generation, but there exists a very real danger that it could prove instrumental in providing a number of undesirable points which were previously non-existent. It is clear therefore, that any out-cross envisaged has to be studied with tremendous care before it is applied. The out-cross mating is one of un-related animals, with no common ancestors involved. When used it is hoped that some desired attribute will be introduced and indeed, the system may well achieve this, but it can just as easily introduce a number of less desirable points taken from either parent or both.

The breeder who plans the use of an out-cross must ensure that the dog to be used is genetically pure with factors capable of correcting the in-bred fault which offends in the bitch. A dog capable of imparting correction which will more or less rectify the fault is a better out-cross proposition than the stud whose bloodlines permit him to more than 'swallow' the fault and by so doing bring to the surface in the progeny some other undesirable feature, hitherto unnoted. Generally out-crossing brings an uneven litter and the good points aimed for in the progeny may well not appear in the mated pairs' first generations, often becoming apparent in the second generation, i.e. the grandchildren.

## Elementary breeding

Any proud owner with a handsome pedigree Boxer will wish to try to reproduce its kind. If it is a stud dog, then he will want to see some good male progeny to adequately continue the line; if a bitch, then a nice uniform litter to suckle some of her virtues from her, and who knows, perhaps grace the winning show benches within a year? A lot of folk become deeply absorbed in dog breeding, especially if they are fortunate enough to achieve success in their early ventures.

The beginner's first lesson in this work is to apply himself to the Boxer breed Standard in relation to the living dog. To learn about the breed, nothing is better than to attend as many shows, especially Championship shows where Boxers are on view, as possible. Here he should watch the judging and in spite of his own novice status in the breed he should endeavour to form his own conclusions as to the relative merits of the competing exhibits. He should not be shy in discussing their points with established breeders present. The leading Boxer kennels should be visited. There he will usually be well received by the proprietors and helped with his problems and queries. Most Boxer breeders are well-disposed to the novice and ready to help him with sound, helpful advice and a great deal can be learnt from the right people. But the newcomer should bear in mind that to commence and finally establish a sound and successful strain will have entailed a great deal of hard work, scheming, financial loss and a lot of disappointments. Therefore, whatever information is given should be received with gratitude, for it is of high value to any novice who is able to use it to avoid the pitfalls into which he would undoubtedly fall without it. On the other hand, he should learn to sort the wheat from the chaff as he listens; not every chance remark should be taken as gospel. Quite a lot of folk, even some with many years in the Boxer breed, still remain quite lacking in factual knowledge. It will pay the student to learn to distinguish between opinions and facts.

Most successful breeders, even those with some knowledge of genetics, have what is known as 'an eye for a dog'. This sense – you could almost term it a gift, is something not everyone is fortunate enough to possess. Those who have it however, are frequently with many years of breed experience too and they rely implicitly upon this instinct when making their decisions. Let it not be thought however, that the man who has had perhaps thirty or more years in a breed is better able to judge or assess a dog's true points than one who has only a few Boxer years to his credit. The latter may well have studied his subject deeper and with greater ability. Nevertheless, it is right to say that length of practical association with Boxers sharpens the eye as to what constitutes a good dog of a given type. There is an old and well-tried breeding law – 'like begets like'. It develops from the method of appraisal normally used by successful livestock breeders when employing the breeding formula of 'Appearance plus Pedigree', already referred to in this chapter. It assumes that when two parents of similar type are mated together their progeny will be of that same type. Successful breeding by this method can be assured *provided* it is supported by efficient line breeding. This has to be based on a clear picture of the parents' ancestry as far back as possible. To achieve this, the mating pairs' pedigrees have to be studied so that each and every ancestor is pictured with its good and bad points. In effect, the pedigrees are made 'eloquent' with ancestral breed history.

To follow the system through to a successful conclusion, you must find a mating pair which resemble each other structurally. They have to be good Boxers, as near to the requirements of the Standard as possible, certainly with no glaring faults. They have to be completely sound anatomically and temperamentally and in first-class health. Never consider any animal with vice or similar temperamental deficiency for a breeding programme and endeavour to ensure that the female family line can claim a series of good and reliable whelpers and bitches strong in mothering qualities. With all such favourable points present you will stand a good chance of producing stock which conforms to the same good type.

When the puppies are bred, it will be found that the majority inherit much of the characteristics of both sire and dam, yet there will be some youngsters in the litter who do not bear much, if any, resemblance to either parent. Thus, assuming that both parents have excellent heads, then it is reasonable to expect that most of the progeny will have good heads, but it is quite likely that a few members of the litter will have weak heads. These could be throw-backs to an early ancestor of whom you may or may not have much information, depending on whether you were able to complete with factual data the members of both parents' genealogical tree. On noting the appearance of youngsters with weak heads, you should be able to refer to your pedigree annotations and no doubt discover that the parental dam's grand-dam (for example) was commented upon for her weak head and skull. This could well mean that the dam of your puppies carries a tendency latently which she can transmit (has transmitted in this instance) in subsequent generations.

When dissimilar types of Boxers are bred together, some puppies will tend to follow one parental type and some the other with possibly one or two falling midway between the two sorts. The latter kind, even if they prove worthwhile specimens, which is unusual, will be of little use to someone with conscientious breeding in mind, for they will pass on to their own progeny the undesirable features of their own parents. Because of this danger alone, the value of knowing a lot about your dogs' pedigrees is apparent. The more you know of their ancestry the better your chances of successful breeding, provided this knowledge is applied intelligently and with the determination to succeed in the drive to produce better Boxers.

## Choosing a bitch

In any mating pair the bitch is of primary importance. The commonly recognised course of inheritance is tail male which considers objectively the sire, the grand-sire, the great grand-sire and so on, when planning a union. In this way the female lines are frequently overlooked, possibly because the task of planning a breeding programme is made easier because the great number of offspring from a male enables the planner to assess better his worth as a sire; whereas the progeny of a bitch is necessarily limited. This preference for a male's influence is unfortunate, for tail female course of inheritance is one of the most important factors in breeding to type, for without good bitches to breed to good dogs, no real or permanent advance towards perfection can ever be made.

It is important that the beginner should buy the best bitch he can afford and this does not necessarily mean the most expensive. Today, there are highly competent and reputable Boxer kennels specialising in show and breeding stock. A few discreet enquiries will quickly ascertain in which establishments the novice can place his faith. It must never be thought that a good bitch's conformation and points are of secondary importance. Certainly, it is important when breeding to select a good sire, but it is *vitally* important to have a good dam.

Whereas with a good bitch one might breed some excellent stock with an ordinary stud dog, even the best of sires is hard put to it to produce something good out of a plain bitch. Good stock will never come from a

Mrs C. Beardsell's
Ch. Newlaithe
Ariadna.

poor female. Admittedly, there have been instances of mediocre dams producing the occasional winner, but these exceptions are of little use to the breed generally for the poor bitch is a 'black mark' in the pedigree of her successful progeny, who will almost inevitably throw back to her at a later date. Most breeders who produce what they believe to be a 'flyer' from sub-average background frequently congratulate themselves prematurely. Such advantages usually turn out to be only temporary.

Some guidance as to how a good bitch should be bought can be given. Not many people can afford a Champion. Not every newcomer to the breed would want to anyway and I am not sure that it is a good thing to try and take too short a cut to the top. It is better to buy an adult bitch or at least a well grown puppy – as free from faults in her make and type as possible. Try and secure one with a pedigree which matches her in good looks. Remember the exhortation 'Appearance + Pedigree' given in earlier pages and you will know what to strive for in your purchase-to-be. Study the living animal first: she *must* have a good head for this is the dominant feature of the Boxer. It is the first part of the overall dog that anyone looks

at. It has to impress and it has to be good and correct. It has to be the main feature of the well-balanced specimen. Take the head and skull in your two hands and explore its contours. Do not be impressed overmuch with exaggeration. A bitch should look feminine so insist on a feminine head. A masculine headpiece on a female would be a fault and to be deplored by any competent judge. A doggy bitch is not quite as bad as a bitchy dog, but both are detested in the breed and must be avoided at all costs. Such a bitch might well produce coarse stock for you and prove useless to any discerning breeder. The nobility of the headpiece should not need looking for – it should stand out at once. If it does not then seek the reason why. It is possible that the cheeks bulge too much and do not fuse well into the muzzle. Maybe the muzzle itself does not tip enough. The point where it joins the frontal skull should be slightly lower than the nose tip when the head is viewed in profile. Check eye emplacement, size and colour of the eyes too. Your understanding of the Boxer breed Standard will be telling you what to seek.

Ears, both their size and set-on will need a check as will dentition and lips.

Mrs A. Norman's Thayman Cinna.

Go right down the neck over the shoulders and ribs back to the croup. Ensure a good symmetrical conformation; seek balance and angulation. Insist on a well coupled animal. Some breeders aver that a bitch can be longer coupled than a dog. This may be, but do not allow too much latitude in this department for in excess a lot will be lost in balance and general appearance. Legs and feet are of great importance too. Any Boxer with poor feet could never express herself when moving – no matter how good she might be in other points, so move her away from you and towards you until you are satisfied she is with good limbs and feet and knows how to use them to her (and your) advantage.

Bone structure is important too. There is an old saying, 'What's bred in the bone will out in the flesh'. This infers that what has been passed down tail female over the generations will always show itself in subsequent generations. Light bone is a transmittable fault. If it exists in your bitch under examination it is unlikely that she will be much use to you; not only will she fail to give good effect if you show her, but her offspring will either show similar weakness or carry the fault through to their own progeny.

Examine her tail. It has to be set on right and in the right place too. A tail set on too low completely detracts from a Boxer's visual effect. One longer than the required two inches will spoil her body profile and rear balance too.

The main thing is that you should take your time making this assessment. Never be hurried into your selection. If the owner of the bitch appears to be impatient or attempts to influence your choice with sales talk or similar, best let the bitch go elsewhere. Any reputable kennel will understand your desire to ensure a good bitch for your foundation; in fact, a breeder might well welcome the purchaser who wants to make up his or her own mind; at least it decides where the responsibility will rest.

Given ample time then, you can assess the Boxer bitch's character and temperament. If she seems cowed, she is no good, even though you might prove able to reassure her at a later date, for the damage has been done. If she lacks verve and cheerfulness, you might wish to know why. One does not want a Boxer which fusses over every stranger, but most of the Bull Breeds are 'matey' to use an apt expression, and you can expect at least some friendliness and good nature to be expended upon you. See how alert she is, how watchful, how ready for a game. Is she well endowed with Boxer breed type? The possession of this attribute is essential to an animal required for exhibiton and breeding.

Lastly, you must check on the bitch's mothering capacity. If she comes from a female family of good whelpers, bitches noted for their instinctive skill at producing and rearing puppies, then your specimen under review stands a very good chance of following in her forebears' footsteps. Of course, if she is already the mother of puppies then a few tactful enquiries about the way she whelped them will help you in your final decision. On the other hand, if she is a maiden, then only time will tell you how she is geared to raise puppies. Should there be some doubt as to her ability at the task then avoid her at all costs, for a bad mother can be a worry as well as an expense. Further, such a bitch is quite capable of begetting daughters who will prove poor mothers in their turn.

## Buying a puppy

If you have very little money to spend on your new bitch then the best plan is to consider the purchase of a puppy of the choicest possible breeding and rear her yourself. The points to look for in a puppy of say three months are : (a) good head with average amount of wrinkle; in effect, neither too much nor too little. The head should be square, the skull deep through, the stop quite well defined. This latter point carries importance and it should be sought in conjunction with a short, square and deep muzzle. (b) ears which are well set on the skull and of medium texture when taken between finger and thumb. Heavy hound-type ears are not wanted although American fanciers generally can obviate poor ear appearance by cropping, a procedure forbidden in Britain. (c) strong rounded ample bone, (d) good size for age; a smallish Boxer is seldom of use to the discerning breeder, a brood bitch especially being required in quite generous proportions, (e) a sprightly temperament, (f) good pigmentation. A poor colour fawn or an indistinct 'muzzy' brindle is useless to the conscientious breeder, for it is transmittable and will appear in any offspring bred from the animal. Keep to the requirements mentioned and you will avoid such effects on subsequent progeny.

Place the puppy you like on a table, examine her in silhouette against a clear background. Her body should be 'squarish' when seen in profile which means that her couplings are good. Her stance should be firm and her chest deep, her neck clean, fore limbs straight and hind legs telling you that they are shaping up for true Boxer angulation. Look down upon her and ensure that she is well endowed with rib, giving her plenty of heart and lung room. The shoulders need to be properly placed, the blades being angled well back. Any upright construction of the shoulder blades will interfere with correct Boxer movement, the gait becoming mincing instead of positive in style. Make sure the specimen you have before you is not tucked-up behind. The true Boxer form must never be thus; it is a physical weakness and it may well indicate colic too. No Boxer with tuck-up can possibly move to satisfy a qualified judge of the breed. Your new puppy *must* be sound. This is of paramount importance for no matter how typey the bitch, how attractive to look at, she is useless if unsound, for she will pass on the weaknesses to her progeny and neither they nor she will ever achieve success in the show ring.

Make sure before your final decision that she moves around freely in the

open. View her fore and aft, see her from the side and look down upon her –
in fact, inspect her from every conceivable angle. Be satisfied on each and
every point before you part with your money. Given satisfaction in all
departments, you will stand a good chance of buying and rearing a typical
Boxer. Remember though, that puppy-buying is a gamble, pure and
simple. Your chances of picking a Champion are extremely slender to say
the least!

When you decide to buy, pay for the bitch and take her home. Make sure
that you secure her Pedigree and other documents at the same time. These
should be ready for you and you are entitled to them at time of purchase.

## Choosing the sire

It must never be thought that the wins attributed to a stud dog necessarily
make him a good sire. A lot of breeders are influenced by a dog's show wins,
which may well not be of much value when properly assessed. It is not
unusual for a dog to win his title in quite mediocre competition, or at shows
which are unpopular with exhibitors generally, either by virtue of their
inconvenient geographical location or the policy of the promotors. For this
reason it is essential that the bitch owner visits as many big shows as he can.
There he will find the best of the Boxers in the current year and he will be able
to assess the worth of every win for himself.

A stud dog should be chosen solely for the value of his get (progeny),
rather than for the number of first prizes he has won. It is only by
employing the former rule that you will become a successful breeder. You
may have a good bitch, but she will have some fault; that perfect one has yet
to be bred and it is essential for your own success that you make yourself
aware of these failings. If you are blind to her faults or refuse to accept their
presence then you might as well give up the idea of pedigree dog breeding
forthwith. Only a man who knows the weaknesses in his Boxer can have a
hope of correcting them. It is possible to breed out any deficiency with care
and calculation over a number of generations, according to the intensity of
the fault, but the planning to achieve good results without introducing
faults – hitherto non-existent, is the work of a dedicated breeder.

Some breeders seem to think the way to correct a fault is to utilise a stud
dog endowed with the exact opposite of that fault. For example, suppose
your bitch is rather high on the leg, the theory is that she should be mated to
a dog who is extra low on the leg, in the belief that one extreme will cancel
out the other. In fact, this is no more than mating fault to fault and although
it is quite possible that the odd puppy or two would crop up which fell
midway between the two parental types, the main result of the litter would
be to produce some puppies which were too high on the leg (taking after
their dam) and some which were too low to the ground (taking after their
sire). Worst of all, the whole litter, however they finished up, would

represent indifferent breeding potential when their time came to reproduce, for they would carry the tendency to transmit *both* parents' faults to their progeny. The secret in breeding is to find a stud dog for this bitch who stands the correct height from the ground, then as has been shown, some puppies tend to resemble either parent, you would get several youngsters standing at the correct height. They in their turn would carry the tendency to transmit only *one* fault, viz. legginess, inherited from their dam and not two faults, legginess and shortness. It should be understood that the foregoing illustrates one example, but numerous examples could be given by applying any pair of opposite characteristics.

It is important when choosing a stud dog to ensure that he is a *real* Boxer, handsome, upstanding, typical and masculine; further, that he has shown irrefutably that he can reproduce his own excellent type. It is not difficult to check on this; for he will have produced litters out of other bitches and you should make a point of inspecting as many of his offspring as you can locate. Ensure too that the stud dog you decide upon as a mate for your bitch has the true Boxer temperament. There are some leading studs who lack perhaps, this much-prized characteristic. Some will have won their top awards under judges who have neither recognised nor realised the necessity for maintaining proper breed temperament.

The sire to be selected is one who suits the breeding of your bitch, is as near Boxer perfection as possible and whose ancestry is beyond reproach. He must be sound, healthy, spirited and masculine, teeming with type and quality. The fact that he can claim to be a Champion is of no paramount importance. Never rush to sires because they have attained a title. Certainly, the written pedigree of the puppies will shine brighter than that of puppies with an un-titled sire, but it is puppy *quality* you want first and there are probably worthier Champions out of the show rings you attend than in them. This can be either for reasons of their owners' inability to visit the major shows or their lack of interest in exhibiting.

## Mating

It is not really fair to inflict maternal duties on a Boxer bitch before her second heat, quite apart from the fact that it is not uncommon for one mated earlier to 'miss' or experience whelping complications, likely to spoil her for the future. This might apply specially in the case of females who are immature physically.

The wise breeder will endeavour to have his bitch mated at her second heat. This occurs usually when the animal is about fourteen or fifteen months old. By this time she is normally both physically and temperamentally prepared for the somewhat onerous duties of motherhood. Assuming then that parturition proves successful, the generally adopted pattern from that point onward is to miss a heat, then mate again. This will give the bitch a fair chance to body up and be ready for another family. It is not uncommon to let her have a second family immediately following the first and providing the bitch is A.1. generally, no harm would be done to her constitution. If however, your ambitions with the bitch include making her a show winner, then you will need to plan the breeding more strategically, for a good bitch needs the first two years of her life un-marred by maternal duties if she is to make an impression in the show ring.

It is assumed that having selected a sire for your bitch you will have informed the owner of the probable date for the union. Once she begins to show 'colour' (a bright blood discharge at the vagina) you will have at least a good idea when the mating should occur. You can then inform the owner of a firmer date for the meeting, this being usually twelve days from the first signs of blood. As is commonly known, a bitch's oestrum (or season) extends between sixteen and twenty-one days. Most bitches are ready for mating on the twelfth day, some can be mated almost any time between the tenth and fifteenth day – it will vary according to the individual. There are a few bitches who are awkward enough to come ready for mating only over a very short period, sometimes as brief as a mere few hours in their season. Such females need to be 'caught' at their required time and this is not always easy for the breeder. The best way to achieve results is to arrange for her to be kennelled near to the sire. Then, when she is ready and willing she will indicate this and the dog can be introduced. However, not many stud dog owners like such bitches, for even an experienced sire quickly wears down and becomes distracted with a bitch in full season next door to his kennel. It is probable that if you own a bitch with such a foible, you will need to find extra fees and/or charges in order to accomplish her final mating. However, if she is a good one and capable of producing something really promising then the extra trouble and expense will doubtless prove worthwhile.

In normal mating arrangements it is considered usual to take the bitch to the dog. However, if he resides at a distance you may be forced to send her to him by rail. This will require careful arranging. She will need a good strong, roomy box and every detail of the journey must be planned carefully; also, the stud dog owner must be informed precisely what you have done so he can be prepared his end. Sending a crated bitch is always a hazardous procedure. The bitch, being in season, is bound to be a bit nervous. She will not like being sent off alone to a strange home, to encounter a bombastic stud dog and to fret about the family circle she has just left. Bitches reduced to this state of mind frequently 'miss' and this will put an end to breeding hopes with her for at least six months. It is better to accompany her to the stud dog, even if this entails you yourself having to spend the night away from home. At least, you will have the personal satisfaction of knowing that you saw the matter through from start to finish.

It is always best to arrange a mating for the early morning, providing both dog and bitch have been allowed ample time to empty themselves. Neither animal should have eaten at least twelve hours before the introduction and the only 'refreshment' allowed down should be a bowl of water. If your bitch is a maiden and the stud dog you have selected for her is experienced, it is likely that all will go smoothly, for the dog will be well versed in the art of courtship. If on the other hand, the stud dog is an untried one, then with a maiden bitch involved, the situation can become ludicrous and some care must be taken. Such a stud dog in his excitement, will probably rush around all over the place, acting so stupidly that the bitch will be put ill at ease and either go for him or completely refuse to co-operate with him. At such a mating, at least two handlers are recommended, one of whom should have some useful experience of mating procedure. The bitch's owner should be at her head end – holding her collar firmly. The best way to do this is to put the thumbs under the collar on either side of her head, then clasp the leather band and if her ears are taken in as well, so much the better. In this way the wrists can be rested against her cheeks to steady her and prevent her turning round to savage the dog as he mounts her. Some breeders muzzle a difficult bitch with conventional muzzle or tape at mating time, but this is a drastic method and not to be recommended unless as a last resort. Not only does it constitute almost a cruelty, but even a savage bitch seems affected adversely by a forced mating. Assuming the bitch to be mated is being held comfortably and being spoken to in soothing fashion by her owner, and that she is ready for the union, no trouble need be encountered. The second handler should support her rear end by putting his hand and forearm beneath her loins. The stud dog, if he is experienced, will at once mount her, but if he is not, then he may need some encouragement to proceed, also it may prove necessary to give him some manipulative assistance by guiding him to the bitch's vulva. Such early training with novice stud dogs is extremely valuable to them. They speedily pick up the idea and their affairs thereafter are conducted with the minimum of delay and the maximum efficiency. Even the old hand at the game appreciates human co-operation at times when the going is tough with an awkward bitch, some stud dogs even expecting a bitch to be held for them to make easy entry!

Occasionally, you will meet breeders who prefer and recommend 'natural' mating. This means that the dog and bitch in season are left alone to their own devices, perhaps in a room or outhouse. It is expected that they will effect copulation unaided, and of course, this sometimes happens. If it does, then it saves a lot of bother, but unfortunately, such matings are seldom achieved without some distress being caused to one of the partners in the union and for this reason alone a well-conducted and supervised mating is considered preferable. Pedigree Boxers are valuable creatures and strong though they may be, there is little sense in allowing two powerful animals, one of them determined, the other timid, unattended, where they can do themselves an enormous amount of harm. Such calamities as slit ears, gashed eyes and ruptured studs can occur easily enough, even in a mating pair quite used to each other in normal circumstances.

The stud dog's natural instinct will cause him to take the initiative in the mating. Once he has effected entry to the bitch, her rear end handler should hold him there a few moments, meanwhile steadying her even more to ensure that she does not try to eject him. These few moments should allow a 'tie' to be achieved and this will indicate conclusively that seminal fluid is being deposited. This 'tie' is important in that it confirms a satisfactory mating. It is not essential to one, however, and many litters are conceived without one. The usual time for a 'tie' to run is between fifteen and thirty minutes. It is not uncommon for breeders to balance the length of a 'tie' with the ultimate success of a mating, believing that the longer the pair are tied the more puppies will result. This is a fallacy. From the commencement of the 'tie' the two animals will have endeavoured to bring themselves tail-to-tail, the accepted position for canine intercourse. However, should it seem that they are struggling to gain this position, yet with little success, some help can be given them by the handlers. One should steady the bitch's head and body, the other handler meanwhile gently easing and swivelling the male round, lifting one of his legs up and over the bitch's back, while his two forelegs are together on the ground alongside her. His head and foreparts should be gradually brought round to the rear and his lifted leg will follow round and eventually join the other hind leg down on the ground. It will then be found that both animals are brought tail-to-tail and perfectly comfortable. Even so, the watch on them should not be relaxed until the dog disengages the bitch, for she is capable of becoming bored with the affair and might drag him backwards while the union is taking effect. When the dog is free from her he should be removed from her presence and left in a quiet room or kennel to regain his composure. The matter of his personal comfort can be attended to by ensuring that the sheath has returned to its natural position covering the penis. Both animals should be watered and rested after adequate feeding. It is considered normal to allow one mating only when the sire is used regularly at stud; for an untried dog it is better to let him mate again with the bitch within say thirty-six hours of the first mating. It could be that the first service will have done little but stimulate the second (and effective) mating, hence this precaution.

In conclusion, some explanation as to the 'workings' of a 'tie' might be appreciated by readers of this book. It occurs when the dog is at his highest state of sexual excitement, i.e. when he has entered her to the extent of his final thrust and is pumping something like several million sperm into her. At this stage his penis will have undergone some change. It will have swollen to three or four times its normal size and the bulb which is a rather hard swelling not unlike the size and shape of a ping-pong ball, situated half way along the length of the penis, will hold the pair together, 'tied' in effect, until that bulb deflates when the union concludes.

Some fanciers have wondered why dog and bitch come tail-to-tail when mating. It is believed that the position is some provision by Nature for a mating pair in the wild state. A dog and bitch so occupied and placed in this way have biting armament at both ends; not only this, but they can travel the armament in a complete circle! Thus, any attacker at such an inconvenient time can be reasonably well withstood and the pair are far less vulnerable than if their backs were turned against any onslaught.

**The bitch in whelp**

Many breeders prefer to worm their bitches prior to a mating. It cannot be a bad idea and this being so, administer a reliable vermifuge or veterinarily recommended medicine not later than one week after the finish of her season. The normal period of gestation is sixty-three days, although deliveries before as well as after the expected date are by no means uncommon. A bitch whelping for the first time is prone to early litters, even as much as five days. When such occurs, the puppies should be treated as requiring five days longer than normal to pick up lost ground in maturity.

Exercise of the bitch in whelp should be normal up to within a fortnight of the expected whelping date. After this time the walks should be easier and perhaps slower. Such things as jumping and rough play should be discouraged and her feeding should be such as to maintain her good condition and allow enough extra nourishment (including calcium phosphate sources) to help with development in the puppies to come. It has been found useful with a bitch shortly to whelp to give a small teaspoonful of medicinal paraffin every day. This will keep her bowels open and oil her up nicely inside. This course is a short one and need not commence much before ten days prior to her expected whelping date. Just before the date of her whelping her food should be reduced a little and the feeds should be staggered. There is no reason to envisage any difficulties arising with the whelping, especially if the bitch is from a sound, acknowledged good whelping family of bitches. However, it is always a good thing to be prepared for the occasional 'situation' which might prove awkward, and forewarned on likely embarrassments is to be forearmed with the remedy.

For this reason at least, it is important to provide a suitable whelping box. This will allow the bitch to have her puppies comfortably and in circumstances whereby they will be afforded the maximum security from accidents. The whelping box shown in the accompanying sketch will be found ideal for the average breeder and it is designed to prevent accidents and to allow the owner ever facility in attending his bitch. The 'pig-rail' is

Whelping box: The size can be adjusted to suit individual needs, but a suitable floor area for the Boxer is 9 sq. ft. The 'pig-rail' will prevent puppies being flattened by an awkward dam. It should be raised about 5″/6″ from floor level and project about 4″ from box side. The lid when closed will allow the bitch to escape her puppies during the weaning period and the draw-bridge side can be lowered at will to control the puppies movements when they are at walking stage.

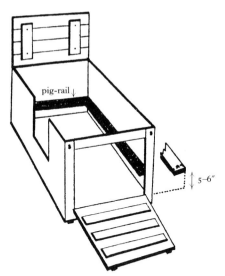

an important feature of the design; it has prevented many a puppy being squashed by a clumsy dam. The extent of the rail or ridge should be enough to allow ample room for a puppy to rest beneath it, even with the bitch's body against it. The lid when closed, makes a suitable ledge for the dam to jump upon when she wishes to avoid the attentions of her brood, during the weaning period at least. The specially designed drop-front will allow the puppies' comings and goings to be controlled effectively. Naturally, the dimensions given are open to modification according to your specific requirements and the whole design of the box can be improved to suit yourself.

It is better to dispense entirely with box bedding while the bitch is actually whelping. If she is made comfortable to the extent of allowing her blankets or soft base material, her puppies could suffer by being enveloped in the folds of the cloth and smothered. If you must use bedding, then a disinfected, clean piece of hessian or crash material is best. This should be nailed securely to the base of the box with strong-flat-headed nails which cannot be dislodged when the bitch in her labour begins to scratch. Thick layers of hay or straw should be avoided for the same reason as given for blankets and soft linings. The bitch is best introduced to her whelping box and quarters a good week before the event. By the time she whelps she will have become used to her new surroundings away from the family circle and commence her maternal duties without any distractions. Her temperature when about to whelp will usually drop to below 100 degrees F., even to 97.5 degrees F. This should be a fair indication to the breeder that labour pains are imminent. The bitch will probably refuse food and drink at this stage and show some agitation in preparing her nest, scratching and swivelling around on herself in typical pre-whelping fashion. Just before she whelps she may well relax into a profound sleep, this being Nature's way of preparing her for the onerous period ahead.

STARTING TO WHELP

The careful breeder will have prepared himself for the whelping by providing himself with a good first-aid kit. What this comprises is entirely up to him in that it covers essential helps to the bitch during delivery, and what his experience tells him he will need. To the complete novice, a good guide would be:

1. A fresh packet of soft paper napkins or squares of surgical lint, about eight inches square.
2. A pair of sharp, sterilised probe-pointed surgical scissors.
3. A quantity of surgical thread or strong cotton.
4. 'Vaseline', also 'Dettol', also 'T.C.P.' or similar antiseptic.
5. Some clean, dry pieces of towelling.
6. A covered hot water bottle, preferably a stone one.
7. An emergency feeding bottle.
8. A quantity of brandy, which if required should be given sparingly, a drop or two at a time in a teaspoon.

The bitch when about to whelp will have gone off her food; a slight straining or rippling will be observed along the contour of her back. This will become more frequent and the reflexing more acute until there are three or four strains every five minutes. Probably by this time the first warm milk drink should be given to the bitch to hasten progress, although very often best results are achieved by leaving her alone. If however, the animal is already very late in producing her puppies and the breeder is experiencing some real anxiety as to her welfare then it will be wise to call in the veterinary surgeon. Puppies are born one by one.

In a normal confinement, the first water bag will have appeared at the entrance to the vulva. This is a small water-filled membranous sac about the size of a tennis ball. It acts as a cushion buffer or protector to the oncoming puppy against pressure and the dam with her licking and straining will break its surface. The initial puppy birth should take place almost at once. If it does not then the breeder should be on his guard and be ready to call in his veterinary surgeon without delay.

Assuming that the puppy does make its appearance within a reasonable time, it will be presented head first, this being the normal delivery; however, those that come rear end first need occasion no alarm unless the dam seems to be distressed in which case she will need assistance. Rear end first birth is known as breech birth and can prove awkward, although it is more serious with the brachycephalic breeds such as Pekinese, Pugs, etc., members of the large headed, flat faced breeds with small pubic apertures. Every birth has to be assessed on its merits or demerits. This is when a breeder's experience will tell him what action to take. Any form of interference during whelping is undesirable and it is best always to let Nature take its course. Only when it is sensible to assume that the situation looks critical should veterinary help be employed.

Maiden bitches need special attention. Occasionally, a maiden will panic at the sight of her first puppy, or be frightened at her labour pains, hitherto unexperienced. Sometimes a bitch will make no effort to produce her puppies and will lie dormant when the first puppy appears at her hind end. If this happens, the breeder should take up one of the pieces of clean towelling he has ready and grip gently the newborn and ease it out of its dam in rythym with the strains. The experienced bitch will break the sac, but whatever happens the youngster must be allowed air into its lungs or it will expire.

Once out of the sac, it must be encouraged to breathe by either its mother's vigorous tongue applying what is really a form of artificial respiration or by the breeder's firm massaging of its body. The dam should nip the umbilical cord which connects the whelp to the placenta (or afterbirth) which will still be inside her. If she does not it must be done for her and this is achieved by taking the cords between finger and thumb and gently pulling it so that the placenta is withdrawn from the mother. Take care that no pull is made from the direction of the puppy itself. Any tug away from the youngster's navel may well cause an umbilical hernia which apart from being a disfigurement in later life might necessitate a minor operation to disperse it. Then the surgical scissors should be taken and the cord severed just above where it has been tied with a piece of surgical cord. This should be at a point about one and half inches away from the puppy's navel.

The placenta can then be disposed of, although in wild life and where the bitch is satisfactorily conducting her own deliveries, it is likely that she will devour the afterbirths. This is an instinctive action, no doubt a heritage from the wild state where they would constitute an emergency meal or even reveal her presence to some marauding carnivore to whom she and her brood would form an easy prey. A lot of breeders do not allow their bitches to dispose of the placentae in this way, either from reason of distate for the idea or because to the modern domestic Boxer some biliousness might result. The matter is relatively unimportant and is only mentioned to save the owner any worry should the bitch dispose of the afterbirths in this way. Actually, it is best to retain them away from her while she whelps for at the end of the whelping session they can be counted against the number of puppies present. In this way, it can be checked that no afterbirth remains in the bitch, for it could result in infection with complications for the animal, as well as arrest the progress of the puppies now dependent upon her.

The veterinary surgeon if required to expel a retained placenta will inject Pituitrin which is usually effective in such circumstances. Between deliveries of the puppies the dam will probably have short sleeps; these will replenish her strength for the next bout of straining. Should she appear to slacken her efforts and the straining become distinctly weaker, this might mean uterine inertia necessitating a Caesarian operation. However, Boxers are not particularly prone to such things and providing the bitch is well made and from a good, sound whelping strain, the situation should not arise.

AFTER WHELPING

It will be fairly obvious when the bitch has produced her last puppy and is ready to settle down with them. Her whole attitude will have become entirely more relaxed. Let her have a drink of warm milk to which a beaten egg or a little glucose has been added. She should be persuaded to leave her brood and go outside to relieve herself. This is not always an easy task, for the bitch has become at once maternally possessive of her brood and suspicious for their welfare. However, every artifice should be employed to prevent her containing herself, for it she does for too long it will harm her.

While she is away, her puppies can be examined to ensure they are normal, i.e. without deformities, cleft palate and so on, also checked for sex. Now is probably the time to decide what is to be done with any bad coloured puppies which have turned up, such as all-whites and checks. Frankly, it is better to dispose of these humanely, for they are of little use except as pets without pedigree and will do nothing useful for the conscientious Boxer breeder. The ideal litter numbers five to six. Five is better for they thrive remarkably well on the average milk supply, whereas bigger litters not only absorb more from the dam's constitution, but are slower to develop. Close attention must be given to the weaker members to ensure that they are not ousted from the main teats (inguinals) by the stronger puppies.

As soon as the dam returns to the litter she should be cleaned up and her whelping box put in good order. There is bound to be a good deal of mess and she will probably appreciate these attentions. Suckling should commence almost at once and the little family should be left temporarily to their own devices in a darkened room, quiet and unmolested by children or other animals. The bitch will be exhausted by her earlier efforts and it will allow her an opportunity to orientate herself.

If the litter has proved a large one and it is felt that the bitch cannot cope properly with it, or looks like being an indifferent mother, then a foster parent will have to be considered. The canine weekly journals usually indicate where these can be obtained and certain kennels are noted for their clean and reliable fosters. The Collie breeds are particularly well endowed with milk and make good fosters, but whether pure-bred or mongrels, their breeding is unimportant so long as ample milk is flowing to rear the Boxer youngsters who will have to depend on their new mother. The foster should be introduced to the surplus puppies or the entire litter, as the case may be, as quickly as possible after the whelping.

## Tails and dew claws

Young Boxers want their tails docked when they are about four days old, and the job is best done by a qualified veterinary surgeon who is acquainted with breed requirements in Boxers. The tail should be cut neatly and firmly, preferably at the second joint from the set-on. The tail skin should be drawn right back to the set-on before the cut is made, so that when cut and released it will elasticate back, just partially beyond the wound stump, its edges protecting the raw end and helping it to heal. Sterilise the wound immediately, using either Friar's Balsam or crushed permanganate of potassium crystals. Not much bleeding should ensue if the job is done properly. (See also K.C. Information Leaflet No. 8.)

Dew claws can be removed at the same time. These are the rudimentary digits on the insides of the puppy's forelegs; sometimes they appear on the insides of the hind-legs too, but the latter are objectionable, in the writer's opinion, and no breeder proud of his stock – and most are, likes to find them. Boxer breeders like to remove all dew claws. With them off, the dog's front has a cleaner, more positive line, quite apart from the fact that in later life such appendages if allowed to remain can prove a nuisance by getting caught up in thicket or wire netting and torn. Care should be taken that all wounds made by removal of dew claws and tail docking are checked twice daily until they have healed.

## Post-whelping characteristics

Sometimes a bitch becomes very excitable after she has delivered her puppies. She will whine and appear nervous and uneasy, often panting and transporting her puppies in her mouth from place to place without any apparent reason. The usual treatment for such symptoms is to confine the bitch and her puppies to a darkened room and administer something like Collo-Cal-D, a preparation strong in Calcium and Phosphorus, combined with Vitamin-D. This curbs excitability and replaces calcium deficiencies.

Very often, the breeder himself is to blame for his bitch's state of mind for he has allowed his own anxiety and nervousness to be transmitted to her. It is better for a nervous breeder to keep well away from the scene of the whelping and immediate post-whelping programming. A bitch quickly picks up anxiety and nervousness from her owner, so people likely to cause this condition are probably best advised to leave all such matters with relatives or friends who do not. The average whelping bitch will usually be much too occupied with her new and interesting duties to worry much about her owner's temporary retirement from the scene. A head put round the door at intervals to give her a cheerful word of encouragement will usually suffice!

## Feeding the nursing bitch

For the first day, possibly the second day too, according to her motions, whether loose or not, the bitch should have only nourishing milk diet. There are a number of excellent milk foods available on the market, Casilan being a good example. Give her five milky meals the first day, then come on to a little raw meat, providing her temperature is normal. If this does not remain constant, then back to milky food she must go. A suitable diet for the nursing mother is as follows, the times of course, can be adapted to convenience:

7 a.m. Milk diet such as Casilan drink.
10 a.m. Raw meat
1 p.m. Scrambled or poached egg, also wheatmeal bread
4 p.m. Milk diet as at 7 a.m.
7 p.m. Raw meat or carefully boned boiled or steamed white fish.
10 p.m. Milk diet as at 7 a.m. and 4 p.m.

It must be remembered that feeding has not only to satisfy the bitch, but to charge her with goodness which she can pass down to her puppies. A bitch with a full complement of puppies will need proportionately more food than one with just two or three youngsters to feed. To aid her milk supply, clean cold water and raw fresh meat are the best producers. Keep check on her every day for signs of diarrhoea, common enough following whelping. This can frequently be alleviated by cutting down the volume of milk and giving more water. On the other hand, it is wise to ease off her meat intake too.

The following is a Chart worked out on the sixty-three day basis.

TABLE SHOWING WHEN A BITCH IS DUE TO WHELP

| Served Jan. Whelps March | Served Feb. Whelps April | Served March Whelps May | Served April Whelps June | Served May Whelps July | Served June Whelps Aug. | Served July Whelps Sept. | Served Aug. Whelps Oct. | Served Sept. Whelps Nov. | Served Oct. Whelps Dec. | Served Nov. Whelps Jan. | Served Dec. Whelps Feb. |
|---|---|---|---|---|---|---|---|---|---|---|---|
| 1 5 | 1 5 | 1 3 | 1 3 | 1 3 | 1 3 | 1 2 | 1 3 | 1 3 | 1 3 | 1 3 | 1 2 |
| 2 6 | 2 6 | 2 4 | 2 4 | 2 4 | 2 4 | 2 3 | 2 4 | 2 4 | 2 4 | 2 4 | 2 3 |
| 3 7 | 3 7 | 3 5 | 3 5 | 3 5 | 3 5 | 3 4 | 3 5 | 3 5 | 3 5 | 3 5 | 3 4 |
| 4 8 | 4 8 | 4 6 | 4 6 | 4 6 | 4 6 | 4 5 | 4 6 | 4 6 | 4 6 | 4 6 | 4 5 |
| 5 9 | 5 9 | 5 7 | 5 7 | 5 7 | 5 7 | 5 6 | 5 7 | 5 7 | 5 7 | 5 7 | 5 6 |
| 6 10 | 6 10 | 6 8 | 6 8 | 6 8 | 6 8 | 6 7 | 6 8 | 6 8 | 6 8 | 6 8 | 6 7 |
| 7 11 | 7 11 | 7 9 | 7 9 | 7 9 | 7 9 | 7 8 | 7 9 | 7 9 | 7 9 | 7 9 | 7 8 |
| 8 12 | 8 12 | 8 10 | 8 10 | 8 10 | 8 10 | 8 9 | 8 10 | 8 10 | 8 10 | 8 10 | 8 9 |
| 9 13 | 9 13 | 9 11 | 9 11 | 9 11 | 9 11 | 9 10 | 9 11 | 9 11 | 9 11 | 9 11 | 9 10 |
| 10 14 | 10 14 | 10 12 | 10 12 | 10 12 | 10 12 | 10 11 | 10 12 | 10 12 | 10 12 | 10 12 | 10 11 |
| 11 15 | 12 15 | 11 13 | 11 13 | 11 13 | 11 13 | 11 12 | 11 13 | 11 13 | 11 13 | 11 13 | 11 12 |

| Served Jan. | Whelps March | Served Feb. | Whelps April | Served March | Whelps May | Served April | Whelps June | Served May | Whelps July | Served June | Whelps Aug. | Served July | Whelps Sept. | Served Aug. | Whelps Oct. | Served Sept. | Whelps Oct. | Served Oct. | Whelps Dec. | Served Nov. | Whelps Jan. | Served Dec. | Whelps Feb. |
|---|---|---|---|---|---|---|---|---|---|---|---|---|---|---|---|---|---|---|---|---|---|---|---|
| 12 | 16 | 13 | 16 | 12 | 14 | 12 | 14 | 12 | 14 | 12 | 14 | 12 | 13 | 12 | 14 | 12 | 14 | 12 | 14 | 12 | 14 | 12 | 13 |
| 13 | 17 | 14 | 17 | 13 | 15 | 13 | 15 | 13 | 15 | 13 | 15 | 13 | 14 | 13 | 15 | 13 | 15 | 13 | 15 | 13 | 15 | 13 | 14 |
| 14 | 18 | 15 | 18 | 14 | 16 | 14 | 16 | 14 | 16 | 14 | 16 | 14 | 15 | 14 | 16 | 14 | 16 | 14 | 16 | 14 | 16 | 14 | 15 |
| 15 | 19 | 16 | 19 | 15 | 17 | 15 | 17 | 15 | 17 | 15 | 17 | 15 | 16 | 15 | 17 | 15 | 17 | 15 | 17 | 15 | 17 | 15 | 16 |
| 16 | 20 | 17 | 20 | 16 | 18 | 16 | 18 | 16 | 18 | 16 | 18 | 16 | 17 | 16 | 18 | 16 | 18 | 16 | 18 | 16 | 18 | 16 | 17 |
| 17 | 21 | 18 | 21 | 17 | 19 | 17 | 19 | 17 | 19 | 17 | 19 | 17 | 18 | 17 | 19 | 17 | 19 | 17 | 19 | 17 | 19 | 17 | 18 |
| 18 | 22 | 19 | 22 | 18 | 20 | 18 | 20 | 18 | 20 | 18 | 20 | 18 | 19 | 18 | 20 | 18 | 20 | 18 | 20 | 18 | 20 | 18 | 19 |
| 19 | 23 | 20 | 23 | 19 | 21 | 19 | 21 | 19 | 21 | 19 | 21 | 19 | 20 | 19 | 21 | 19 | 21 | 19 | 21 | 19 | 21 | 19 | 20 |
| 20 | 24 | 21 | 24 | 20 | 22 | 20 | 22 | 20 | 22 | 20 | 22 | 20 | 21 | 20 | 22 | 20 | 22 | 20 | 22 | 20 | 22 | 20 | 21 |
| 21 | 25 | 22 | 25 | 21 | 23 | 21 | 23 | 21 | 23 | 21 | 23 | 21 | 22 | 21 | 23 | 21 | 23 | 21 | 23 | 21 | 23 | 21 | 22 |
| 22 | 26 | 23 | 26 | 22 | 24 | 22 | 24 | 22 | 24 | 22 | 24 | 22 | 23 | 22 | 24 | 22 | 24 | 22 | 24 | 22 | 24 | 22 | 23 |
| 23 | 27 | 24 | 27 | 23 | 25 | 23 | 25 | 23 | 25 | 23 | 25 | 23 | 24 | 23 | 25 | 23 | 25 | 23 | 25 | 23 | 25 | 23 | 24 |
| 24 | 28 | 25 | 28 | 24 | 26 | 24 | 26 | 24 | 26 | 24 | 26 | 24 | 25 | 24 | 26 | 24 | 26 | 24 | 26 | 24 | 26 | 24 | 25 |
| 25 | 29 | 26 | 29 | 25 | 27 | 25 | 27 | 25 | 27 | 25 | 27 | 25 | 26 | 25 | 27 | 25 | 27 | 25 | 27 | 25 | 27 | 25 | 26 |
| 26 | 30 | 27 | 30 | 26 | 28 | 26 | 28 | 26 | 28 | 26 | 28 | 26 | 27 | 26 | 28 | 26 | 28 | 26 | 28 | 26 | 28 | 26 | 27 |
| 27 | 31 | 28 | 1 | 27 | 29 | 27 | 29 | 27 | 29 | 27 | 29 | 27 | 28 | 27 | 29 | 27 | 29 | 27 | 29 | 27 | 29 | 27 | 28 |
| 28 | 1 | 29 | 2 | 28 | 30 | 28 | 30 | 28 | 30 | 28 | 30 | 28 | 29 | 28 | 30 | 28 | 30 | 28 | 30 | 28 | 30 | 28 | 1 |
| 29 | 2 | | | 29 | 31 | 29 | 1 | 29 | 31 | 29 | 31 | 29 | 30 | 29 | 31 | 29 | 1 | 29 | 31 | 29 | 31 | 29 | 2 |
| 30 | 3 | | | 30 | 1 | 30 | 2 | 30 | 1 | 30 | 1 | 30 | 1 | 30 | 1 | 30 | 2 | 30 | 1 | 30 | 1 | 30 | 3 |
| 31 | 4 | | | 31 | 2 | | | 31 | 2 | | | 31 | 2 | 31 | 2 | | | 31 | 2 | | | 31 | 4 |

## Hand rearing

This is a task for the dedicated breeder only. Sometimes, as already mentioned, a bitch following delivery of her puppies will have no milk; she may be too ill to care what becomes of the youngsters or refuse to attend them for a variety of reasons. At worst, she might have expired in the course of whelping or because of a Caesarian. The breeder is left then with an orphan litter, crying for milk which is not forthcoming. If he has been prudent and foreseen the situation, he will have arranged for a foster parent to be standing by, but to come by a foster at a moment's notice is no easy task, so the alternative course of action is for the puppies to be hand-fed. This is by no means as simple as it sounds and any person taking on the task must be prepared for at least a month of devoted attention to the puppies and some sleepless night. However, when the course of feeding has been completed and the litter satisfactorily reared, it will be an unusual breeder who does not survey the results with justifiable pride.

'Lactol' is a good stand-by for bitch's milk. Instructions for hand-rearing will be found on the canister, but great care must be taken in the selection of exact quantities recommended, also the actual mixing, as well as the temperature of the feeds and frequency of feeding. A fresh mixture is essential for every meal and especially where a large litter is involved, care must be taken to ensure food temperature is maintained. This is best achieved by keeping a cup of the 'Lactol' mixture standing in a bowl of hot water, which will ensure that when the time comes to feed the last puppy, his or her food will be given at the same required heat as enjoyed by the first feeder.

As soon as the puppy has been fed, wipe his nose gently with a piece of damp cotton wool. This will remove any congealed milk around his nostrils and face. Normally, if the dam was on the scene she would start licking them as soon as they had fed in order to induce urination and the passing of motions. Her wet, warm and busy tongue directed around their private parts would soon achieve this naturally, but as the orphans are without such maternal attentions, the result has to be achieved artificially. To simulate the bitch's method it is necessary to take a wad of cotton wool which has been dampened with *warm* water. Gently stroke over and around the puppies' parts with this and both water and motions will be quickly passed. After this has proved successful, gently smear with 'Vaseline' the anus and vulva or penis of each puppy. It is important to ensure that the puppies intestines do not become blocked so both motions must be passed either before or immediately following a meal. Should any puppy seem distressed, it may prove necessary to ease gently into the rectum for a fractional distance, a well-greased thermometer. This can be expected to encourage the passing of a motion.

If possible always use an infra-red lamp when hand-rearing puppies. This maintains a constant temperature and should be set to give between 75 degrees to 80 degrees, for the first three days, after which time the temperature can be gradually reduced to 60 degrees. This 'easing off' of the warmth is done by raising the lamp slightly higher each day. Make certain the lamp is suspended safely from the ceiling and use a dull-emitter bulb as this type is considered safer when the youngsters open their eyes, about ten days after birth. It is as well to protect the lamp reflector with a wire guard in case a bulb should accidentally break loose and fall on the litter.

It will be realised that puppies who have been deprived of their dam's milk will lack in Colostrum, the protective natural fluid which the bitch produces in her initial flow. The antibodies contained in this immunise the youngsters from birth until they are about nine or ten weeks of age against such virus diseases as Distemper, Hard-Pad, Hepatitis, etc. This deficiency must be replaced artifically and the veterinary surgeon will inject the puppies for their immunisations with Gamahtine (Gamma Globulin), or similar.

A lot of time, a good deal of patience coupled with some frustration, will be spent in hand-rearing one orphan litter. Providing the rules regarding regularity in feeding, correct temperature of food and surroundings, also regular defecation and urination are observed, success can be expected and deserved.

## Nursing problems

EXCESS MILK

It frequently occurs that a nursing mother will produce too much milk for her brood. Probably because the breeder commenced early weaning, the youngsters would take up less of her own food supply and this is liable to cause congestion in the teat area, especially prone being the major inguinal teats at the rear. These become encrusted and inflamed and cause discomfort. The danger exists when the bitch scratches and nibbles at them in her irritation and this can bring up unpleasant abscesses.

As soon as an over-adequate milk supply is noted, the breeder can help the situation by gently milking the teats, meanwhile cutting down her fluid intake. Of course, there is always the possibility that by doing this more milk will be induced to build up, but as the puppies become more lusty, their greediness will increase and they will balance up the situation and absorb the surplus.

In the unfortunate case of a bitch who has lost her puppies, this presents a different problem, but there are a number of drugs to deal with such a matter and the veterinary surgeon will know what to do. If a dam seems to be carrying milk after her puppies have left, this need cause no alarm, for it will usually disperse naturally. On the other hand, dabbing round the teats with methylated spirit soaked on to a pad of cotton wool has been known to hasten the process.

## Lack of milk (Aglactia)

This can prove a worrying situation for the bitch and for the breeder himself. However, it is by no means uncommon for the whelping mother to acquire a high temperature which could persist for even thirty-six hours, when the milk will be unable to get through to pacify the unsettled whelps. If the state persists for longer than six hours it should be dealt with at once. It helps if the puppies are continually put to the bitch's teats where their sucking will sometimes induce the milk to flow. It should be remembered that when youngsters are deprived of the initial milk flow from their dam they also miss the protective colostrum which comes with it. This has been discussed in the section on Hand Rearing and its remedy lies with the veterinary surgeon.

# 4 Feeding

## Weaning

The way puppies are weaned will have a lasting effect on them all their lives. This shows then that it is vitally important to do the job properly and well, especially if strong and healthy Boxers are wanted. A well-reared puppy is thus put on the right path to full health and one so started seldom suffers a set-back, even in the 'tricky' days of his adolescence. The best time to start weaning the Boxer puppy is when he is about three and a half weeks old. This applies to a puppy from an average sized litter of say five or six members. If the litter is perhaps of eight members, then the earlier you can with safety start weaning them after three weeks of age, the better. A lot depends on the milk supply coming through from the dam. If this is adequate then your start can be more gradual. Firstly, they have to be taught to lap. There are a number of good milk preparations on the market, 'Lactol' being an excellent example. Full instructions for its use will be found on the tin and it is adaptable to any age and weight of puppy. Usually a heaped teaspoonful will do as a starter for each puppy and it should be mixed with hot water just off boiling point to the consistency of thick cream then beaten or stirred well until it appears glossy and emulsified. Then it should be brought to the consistency of thin cream by adding more hot water. Four or five teaspoonsful of the mixture should then be put into a clean saucer and the puppy and its food put on to a clean dry towel. Gently push his nose into the mixture. At first he will object to this indignity and splutter and blow into it; then as the taste of it penetrates his consciousness he will show more interest in the food, especially if a little of it is taken on to the tip of the little finger and placed between his lips. Once he has got over the initial difficulty in lapping he will soon learn to take the food. Always serve the 'Lactol' mixture to a puppy at blood heat and try to maintain the temperature of the food by standing it in a pan of hot water during the feeding operation. Once lapping and eating has been taught, the youngsters can be put on firmer foods like light milk puddings, poached egg, minced boiled tripe and finely shredded fresh raw butcher's meat.

So that a good appetite is maintained and the puppies are eager to eat, it is a good plan to make sure they have been off their dam for at least two hours previously. They will then attack the food with gusto and begin to look forward to their menu. Goat's milk can later be introduced instead of cow's milk and its value cannot be over emphasized in view of its high fat and mineral salts content. Up to the first week of solid feeding, no doubt the puppies will have been fed individually, but it will be found by careful guiding that communal feeding can be achieved. To avoid some of the more eager ones falling head first into the food, it is a good idea to raise the bowl perhaps a couple of inches off the ground level. Make sure when feeding a number of lusty puppies that individuals are not allowed to hog the main part of the food. When this is seen, allow the offenders to get a reasonable share, then withdraw them and leave the way clear for the slower ones. An interesting appreciation of the differences between bitch's milk and that of other quadrupeds is shown in Clifford Hubbard's *The Complete Dog Breeder's Manual*, 1954. This is the table:

ANALYSES OF MILK

| Animal | Sugar | Casein, etc. | Fat | Salts | Water |
|--------|-------|--------------|------|-------|-------|
| Dog | 3.1 | 8.0 | 12.0 | 1.2 | 75.5 |
| Goat | 4.75 | 4.0 | 6.25 | 1.0 | 84.0 |
| Cat | 5.2 | 7.9 | 3.65 | 0.9 | 82.35 |
| Cow | 4.85 | 3.75 | 3.7 | 0.6 | 87.1 |
| Sheep | 4.95 | 4.7 | 5.2 | 0.7 | 84.45 |

After ten days of weaning the puppies should be approaching complete independence from their mother; in fact, the greater their solid food intake the less they will depend on her and when they are five weeks of age, her influence upon them should be negligible. She may want to see them once a day, and they will probably rush her and take a snatched drink at her now failing supply, but she will soon want to see them off, for by now their bulk and strength and sharp claws will irritate her. By this time they will be on five proper meals a day, two or three milky ones and two with raw meat. The quantities should be staggered well to avoid distension of the stomach muscles and watch should be kept on the bitch during her occasional visits in case she regurgitates or disgorges her own food to help in the weaning process. This might seem an unsavoury system to humans, but it is a perfectly natural function on the bitch's part and unlikely to do any harm. The main thing to do is to see that the dam gets another meal for after doing this service she is bound to be hungry. In any case, now is the time to start fattening her up. She has put a lot of strength and body into her puppies and this needs replacement. She should be given plenty of good, fresh raw meat, eggs, cheese and biscuits too, but her fluid intake should be put to a minimum to help the natural diminishment of the milk supply until it finally disappears.

It is possible too that a tonic will help her and this can be prescribed by your veterinary surgeon. She will speedily get back into full bloom and condition if you do this. A lot of owners forget to work on the bitch so occupied are they with her puppies. To do this shows lack of planning skill especially if she is to be mated again at her next heat. Novice breeders are frequently puzzled as to the *amount* of meat to give the young puppy. As a rough, but good guide the amount given at each meal should not exceed the bulk of each puppy's head. Imagine the food lightly shaped or moulded into a ball roughly equivalent in size to the youngster's head and skull. When the food is put down watch him eat it. If he goes through the quantity comfortably, then no doubt it suits his appetite. If he pauses, takes a breath, then starts again, it is reasonably certain that this puppy needs only the amount of food up to the point at where he paused.

At six weeks of age, the puppy can have Farley's Rusks, biscuits, etc. as well as his normal diet. Of course, once the youngster has been fed on food other than his dam's milk she will stop cleaning him. This job must be taken on by the breeder who should ensure that any motions left adhering to the anal region are cleaned off with cotton wool swabs to which has been added a few drops of 'T.C.P.' or similar preparation.

Most Boxer puppies are big enough, fit enough and generally ready to go off to their new homes by the time they are eight weeks old. You can, if you wish, stagger their departures, if the dam is still showing interest, so she does not lose them all at once. Always supply the new owners with a helpful diet sheet. Even people who have had previous experience of puppy rearing should have one, for it is easy enough to forget the art, and lists of recommended foods and feeding times are always appreciated. A simple feeding programme for a Boxer puppy up to four months of age is given below.

Three of a fine litter bred by Mrs S. M. Crompton ('Carnbrea').

## Puppy diet sheet

8.30 a.m. Bread and milk, cereal and milk, light porridge, etc. Make sure that the milk is warm, but never hot.

12.30 p.m. Chopped meat meal. Mix with warm gravy made from 'Oxo', 'Bovril' or similar. Broth is ideal. Wholemeal or brown bread rusks* soaked in the gravy or in boiled vegetable liquid can be added.

4.30 p.m. Warm milk meal, or rusk and gravy.

8.30 p.m. Repeat as for 12.30 p.m. (meat meal).

The meat should be chopped into useful sized pieces, not minced. Some breeders shred it, but it has better results when it brings the dog's gastric juices into play. A dog does not masticate his food like a human. Most of the breaking-up and dissolution of the food is effected by strong gastric juices in his stomach. Minced meat hardly allows the digestive system full play; although even more care is required to ensure the meat is not chopped too chunkily, for this could cause choking.

While the puppy is young it will help bone formation by sprinkling a little powdered calcium on his food. Your veterinary surgeon or chemist will advise on a good form to use; this being put over the puppy's evening meal. do not give ordinary vegetables to a puppy under six months of age, although vegetable juice extract obtained by cooking carrots, endives and turnip tops, poured over a meal is first-class for Vitamin-A application as well as being rich in iodine and mineral salts.


## Adult feeding

Good feeding is an investment. One sometimes hears breeders bemoaning the cash outlay, but they little realise that a dog ill-fed and poorly reared is likely to cost them far more in money and worry at the veterinary surgeon. The aim in feeding is to develop and preserve the dog in good health, in good bloom and with an equable and contented frame of mind. Therefore, the food must be balanced, varied and of the highest standard.

From the age of six or seven months, the forward puppy can be fed as an adult. The best form of feeding is to give one main meal in the evening, possibly with a few dry biscuits at midday. Cool, fresh water should be down for him to drink always. With a youngster, such as one seven months old, it might be deemed wise to allow him a little meat extra to his biscuits at midday, but concentration should always be on the evening repast. This should be rather late in the day, *after* his exercise or field work. Managed this way, he will gain the full nutritive effects of his food while sleeping and its digestion will be orderly. Always feed a Boxer dry, for soft mushy food is

*Rusks can be made from bread by baking slices in the oven.

of no use when best results are wanted. Never feed or water after heavy exercise, such as a ratting expedition, a training session or a fight. Let the dog settle first, return to normal respiration, then give him a drink, followed by food if a meal time is approaching.

Many dogs prefer raw meat. Certainly, meat in this form is best for its goodness has not been drained away in cooking. Nevertheless, it is wise to get a dog used to *all* forms of feeding, i.e. raw meat, cooked meat, boiled and steamed fish, proprietary canned meat, processed forms and so on. Avoid horsemeat if possible and meat unfit for human consumption might also prove unfit for your dog, so use these only in an emergency or not at all. A dog fed on a variety of provender does in fact, get used to anything and thus becomes no difficulty to feed. A Boxer raised solely on raw meat is often fastidious and rejects other food after a peremptory sniff. Such dogs frequently prove worrying at a time when it is neither practicable nor convenient to produce what they want. This is why a dog should be trained in feeding, just as he is trained in other things.

If fish is fed and this food has great nutritive value, make sure it is good white fish and has been carefully boned after boiling or steaming. A freshly caught rabbit is good too, but it should be eaten immediately, for the bones are very dangerous after the first day. Never allow the dog to have poultry or game bones; these are needle-like and many a dog has choked on these. The permissible bones are the big marrow or knuckle bones. These keep the teeth in good form and are often appreciated by the puppy having gum pains during teething, as well as by the growing and mature dog. Other foods worth considering include ox and sheep heart, of rather more value than ox cheek and liver. Tripe and the various forms of offal are of average worth only and paunch, the favourite of many breeders, probably because of its cheapness, is of little value when compared to fresh raw meat. Herrings, cooked in a pressure cooker constitute a wonderful food. Liver, when given, should not appear on the menu more than once a week.

During the winter months always pour a teaspoonful of coarse cod liver oil on the dog's food, or maybe he will prefer to lick the measure off a large spoon to avoid spilling. Malt Extract is a good body builder during the cold part of the year, but in summer months he is better with pure olive oil, which is rather less heating. An adult Boxer needs at least $1\frac{1}{2}$ lb. of raw meat daily, certainly not less than 1 lb. in which event the balance should be made up with some other form of nourishing food, well-endowed with protein, carbohydrates and fats. Meat, eggs, fish and cheese, etc. supply the protein; cereal, biscuits, bread, etc. the carbohydrates, while fats will come from the usual sources: milk, butter content, fish oils, meat fat, etc.

Never economise in feeding, especially a show or breeding dog. A well-fed Boxer in good condition is a prized possession. The goodness you put in to him will strengthen his resistance to disease and show its good effect in the bone and musculation of his progeny.

## Vitamins

Vitamins are essential to the dog's full health. They are present in natural feeding or in sunshine. In the right amounts they give the dog's body all the basic nutrients he needs for goodness and contentment. Modern feeding however, is sometimes suspect and one is inclined to doubt its efficacy in this respect. Certain diseases and conditions are caused by lack of the requisite vitamins and the conscientious Boxer owner should acquaint himself with some knowledge of the worth and effect of vitamins.

*Vitamin A.* This is found in fish liver oils, heart and liver, eggs and milk. It is necessary for healthy skin, healthy bones and teeth and to build up resistance against infection. It can counteract eye conditions, especially 'night-blindness' which is an inability to accept light after a period of darkness and vice versa. Raw carrots and parsley are rich in Vitamin A.

*Vitamin B.* Usually referred to as B-Complex, embracing a number of factors. It exists in milk, meat and eggs, liver, yeast and wheat germ. It strengthens the digestion, aids the nervous system and keeps the dog's skin and coat in good order and prevents constipation. Cytacon (to be taken orally) and Cytamen (for injecting) are made by Glaxo and represent first-class methods of giving Vitamins B.12 tonics.

*Vitamin C.* Stated to be the 'sunshine' vitamin and obtainable from grass and some berries. It will aid the body to resist infection and is essential for growth, good teeth and gums and healthy skin. Milk too contains this vitamin. Note that it is a water soluble vitamin and is not stored by the body which means that a course entails daily dosage.

*Vitamin D.* This is found in fish oils (especially halibut liver oil), egg yolk, butter and liver. It is another 'sunshine' vitamin and is essential for supporting the two minerals needed for good health – viz. calcium and phosphorus. This useful vitamin is an enemy of rickets and similar bone deficiency conditions.

*Vitamin E.* Wheat germ oil is the main source of this vitamin which has an important bearing on fertility in the dog and bitch. An active stud dog can manage well at his job if he has been reared from puppyhood on Vitamin E, for it will maintain his potency and delay advance of possible sterility. When used with the bitch, the chances of dead puppies or absorbed foetuses during pregnancy will be brought to a minimum. Vitamin E Succinate and Wheat Germ Oil capsules are useful for dosing.

The clever breeder will incorporate a proper balance of vitamins and minerals in his application to preserve good all-round health in his Boxer. So long as the dog is allowed fresh meat, fish, milk and eggs with easy access to sunshine and clean, green grass grazing, he is unlikely to go wrong in health. Some meat fat will benefit him as this is strong in Vitamins A & D. A valuable conditioner is 'Vetzyme' (Phillips Yeast Products) containing vitamins and minerals blended for puppy, dog and bitch alike.

# 5 General Management

**Early lessons**

The true Boxer is a high-powered member of the Bull Breeds family; he is strong, athletic, virile and fully endowed with intelligence and determination. Such a fine temperament needs moulding while in the course of its development and this is why most people prefer a small puppy to an adult, for the former can be trained much more simply and to its owner's specific requirements. Firm training is essential; unfortunately, a lot of owners fail to apply rules and regulations to their dogs until too late. Many think that a small puppy rushing pell-mell about the house, knocking down this, ruining that, is a comic circus turn for the family circle. It might be for a time, but only while the puppy is small – it becomes far from funny when the dog is mature and still untrained.

A poorly trained dog reflects upon his owner's aptitude as a trainer. The first word a young dog must learn is 'No'. It is an easy word to say and easy for a dog to understand in its implication, also most puppies are anxious and willing to learn it. Never thrash a puppy; it is a fatal move in training and not many beaten dogs ever regain confidence in the person who beat them, quite apart from the fact that a beaten dog will seldom respond properly thereafter. Corporal punishment, when required, is better applied with a rolled-up newspaper. Keep it handy always and use it sparingly. It will make a deal of noise, but never hurt. The young dog will not like it, but he is unlikely to resent it. The clap it makes when administered should be synchronised with the word 'No'. In a very short time it will be completely unnecessary to use it – only the word itself will suffice. By this simple method a youngster can be persuaded to stop biting furniture, nibbling ankles and to lie down and stop making a nuisance of himself. Just show him what to do in the simplest, most commonsense method adaptable to the problem and he will learn quite quickly.

**House training**

Training a small puppy to be clean in the home has always been a problem to the new owner; even a deterrent to ownership by some very house-proud people. It need never be, for it is simple to house-break a puppy in a very short time. Puppies of just two months of age sleep a great deal, just like a baby. They should be allowed to do this as often as they wish and children should be taught never to disturb them while they rest. Quite apart from a small dog requiring ample sleep to store up energy, even the mildest natured dog must be hard put to retain good humour when pummelled suddenly out of a deep sleep.

When a puppy has had enough sleep he will open his eyes; as soon as the eyes are open *he will want to urinate*. This is the pattern to watch, for then he should be taken up or guided either to the garden or to his sand tray. If out of doors, then close the door on him and watch him until he has squatted and completed the job. Then open the door and call him in. If on the sand or dirt tray, then keep him within the perimeter of the tray until he has finished, then ceremoniously almost, lift him off.

A few lessons such as this will find the idea well embedded in his mind and before long the instant he opens his eyes from a sleep he will seek the outside terrain or the sand tray to do his business. Be sure to praise him when he is good and only the mildest scold when he is not, for he is bound to make one or two mistakes while learning. Never scold him if he makes a puddle indoors because the door was not opened fast enough to let him get outside. To punish him for something which is really the owner's fault is unfair and will probably cause a set-back in his training.

It is probable that he will forget himself at night in any case. Small puppies are continually making puddles – their bladders are quite weak at two or even three months of age. The best plan is to cover the floor of his pen, or the kitchen where he sleeps with newspapers, then in the morning these can be gathered up and put in the disposal bin with the minimum of fuss. While the youngster is learning to be clean, of course, to leave him in rooms where valuable carpets or curtains exist, would be foolish in the extreme. Any untrained animal should be kept where he can do no damage to property and fitments. If a puppy tears up one's best carpet slippers or rips open a cushion or two, never blame the pup; it is the fault of the person who left him there unattended with such temptation!

## On the lead

The next step is to get the young dog used to collar and lead. Naturally, he should not be taken on to the sidewalk until he has had all his inoculations. Too many hazards exist where older dogs have paraded. Lamp-posts especially, seem to harbour disease, yet they hold a traditional fascination for dogs of all ages. For this reason, it is best to give the puppy his elementary lead training in the home and garden.

A cheap collar should be purchased initially for he will soon grow out of it and it will have to be discarded. Buy the light-weight, narrow, strap-like collar with lead to match. The youngster should be trained to accept his collar by putting it on for short, but progressively longer periods until he finally accepts it. At first, he will probably scratch with irritation, but eventually he will come to tolerate it all day without fuss. By wearing a collar, he will become more manageable but it should be removed at night while he sleeps as left on it will disarrange the smoothness of the coat around the neck.

Later, when he finds the collar comfortable a light lead can be attached to it and he can be encouraged to walk up and down. He will not like the idea very much and will probably emulate a trout on the end of a line, but with some re-assurance he will learn to move composedly back and forth. Do not forget to use a titbit or two in the training, giving him one every time he behaves well. Watch for the puppy which pulls excessively and tries to dash too far ahead of his handler. This will detract from the correct development of the shoulders, quite apart from the annoyance it will give his trainer.

Keep early training to periods of about ten minutes duration to save the puppy getting bored. If he pulls excessively, tap him across the extended muzzle with a rolled-up newspaper. Jerk back the lead at the same time with the command 'Heel' or 'Back'. He will soon learn not to pull. A puppy which drags and digs his feet into the ground, so to speak, has to be encouraged with words and tasty morsels to move forward together with a firm pull on his lead, which will bring him into action. With puppies destined for the show ring, it is wise to train them to move on either side of the handler, but when obedience work is the aim, then always keep him on the handler's left side.

## Exercise

A healthy Boxer needs a lot of exercise. He is quite capable of doing six times the amount his equally healthy owner would seek, and yet be ready for more! Make sure he is never let off his lead where traffic is a hazard. Even the best trained ones sometimes fall foul of fast cars. The open fields and parks are best for free running off the lead. Here a ball game can be held without much fear that the dog will come into trouble. Watch should be kept for other dogs of course, making sure that no mischief is made by or against him. Lakesides are better avoided too, for the Boxer likes a swim, whereas you may not be prepared for a wet dog in your car, or the water itself might be stagnant and bad for his health.

A dog being conditioned for show work needs to be hard. Walk him several miles a day over rough ground, even cinder tracks, for this will harden the feet and pasterns, quite apart from its benefit to the hindquarters. Keep an eye open for hills and slopes. Throw the ball up their inclines and let the dog retrieve it. The 'push' he has to employ in getting to the top will bring up his rear muscles beautifully and keep down to a minimum the length of his toe-nails. Although free running exercise is good for him, exercise on the lead is better. It maintains steadiness and rhythm of gait, which will hold him in good stead when he enters the show ring. He should be trained always to *walk* on the lead – this means that the lead from dog to owner's hand should be slack, never taut. Once the dog gets used to his lead and has learned to anticipate, then enjoy his walks, he will achieve a natural action which must be encouraged.

Never over-walk a young puppy for this can do irreparable damage. Exercise is the second important need to the Boxer, the first being his food, of course. Therefore, when it is pouring down with rain outside, do not be tempted to deprive him of his daily walk. So long as he is dried down well, and towelled properly underneath, he will come to no harm. No one should buy a dog unless he intends to maintain its fitness by feeding the animal properly and giving it ample and regular exercise.

A fat Boxer is neither a delight to look at nor does he enjoy life. A dog gets best results from his exercise when he is walked alone, but clearly an owner with a number of dogs can seldom do this. Often one dog will lead another into trouble; it is quite true that with two dogs one has the nucleus of a pack. If a dog or dogs are walked in public, the handler should be completely in control should an emergency arise. One sometimes sees a small girl out exercising a fine Boxer dog. It is wrong – a grown man should handle him, for then he would be under control as all dogs should be when in public. Indoors, it is a different matter for temptation likely to precipitate a serious incident is unlikely to arise.

## Swimming

Water-shy Boxers are a rarity, although it is not unusual to find a dog, an eager swimmer when it comes to sea or lake, step daintily and fastidiously around a puddle! It is reasonably easy to get any Boxer to take to the water, although with some it is necessary to throw in a stick or ball and exhort them to retrieve it. Should a dog prove obstinate, the best method is to employ a trained and keen water dog (of any breed) as an example to the pupil.

## Guarding the home

Some Boxers are speedier than others in learning this valuable lesson. Most of the Bull Breeds are perhaps a little slow at it, being rather too hail-fellow-well-met in their approach to strangers, even up to the middle of their second year. This should occasion no concern, for when they have learned to guard the home, the ability shown proves the waiting period was well worth while.

A young puppy can have some elementary training in the work providing his owner is prepared to put in a little 'acting' to achieve results. Get someone outside to ring the bell or knock on the door or window. The average puppy will at once cock his head and listen – he is at once surprised and aware. At this point the owner should make the best imitation he can of a dog's bark – 'Woof', he will say, and if 'Woof' is said in a low and menacing tone, all the better! The puppy will probably 'catch on' to this after a few tries and before long as soon as the bell rings or the window tap is heard he will 'Woof' too! Once he has started to bark, he will get enthusiastic, especially if encouraged and the lesson will have sunk in; certainly such lessons are never forgotten.

Remember too, that when the dog is older and likely to appear fearsome to a stranger, he should be taken to the door every time one calls. That is why in the section on lead training, it has been suggested that a strap collar should be maintained on the dog all day. As the owner opens the door with his right hand, he should 'hold back' the dog with his left. The dog will almost certainly be thrusting towards the visitor and the whole effect will be one of the fearsome-looking dog trying to 'get at' the caller! Most would-be intruders when they know a householder has a resident Boxer will divert their attentions elsewhere.

## Bathing

An adult Boxer needs very few baths, a small puppy none. This rule is dependent of course, on the animal not having encountered any obnoxious substance which has made his proximity unpleasant or getting covered with mud. In such cases a bath becomes essential. The dog's coat contains natural oils and too much bathing will remove some of these, it taking quite a few days to return to normal. Regular attention with a brush and comb and houndglove every day is much better (see Grooming). However, when applying the brush, go through the dog carefully from muzzle to tail. Check his eyes, his skin and ears – make sure the body harbours no parasites especially where the tail sets on.

When bathing a Boxer, make sure the water is just warm. An over hot bath will upset the dog and make him quite unco-operative next time you want to put him in the tub. He should not have been fed within two or three hours of being bathed and certainly given a chance to relieve himself first. The wise owner will have made sure that everything he wants for the dog's bath is close to hand. The items required are two rough turkish terry towels, one to soak off the initial moisture the other to remove the dampness and to ensure complete dryness underneath the dog and around his more tender areas. If you can arrange the bath where he has a chance to shake himself, so much the better for then you will soak the towels much less.

A good dog shampoo can be used and today a number of reliable makes exist. Use it according to instructions, but make sure that every vestige is removed when rinsing time is over or the coat may cloy in parts and cause some irritation. Extra care should be given when bringing the shampoo near to his eyes and ears. Some owners smear a little petroleum jelly around the eyes and insert a jelly smeared cotton wool wad in the dog's ears for safety. It seems almost unnecessary to warn owners that all such grease and wads *must* be disposed of when the bath is over. It is vital that the dog is dried-off completely. The parts to heed particularly are soft flesh areas in the underparts, the genitals and between the toes. Rub down well around the loins too. Let the dog remain in even temperature for a while – on no account allow him to go out of doors too soon.

## Grooming

The healthy Boxer in good bloom needs very little grooming, especially if he gets daily application of the brush or houndglove to his coat. However, most exhibitors like to 'dolly' their dogs before a show and a little extra gloss to a dog's coat can do nothing but good. The brush or glove will stimulate his muscles too and make him feel perky – that is why some exhibitors are seen busy with grooming tools even at the ringside! It all helps to bring the dog in 'on his toes'. The best type of brush for the Boxer coat is a semi-harsh bristle. Any good pet supplies shop will advise. A good quality houndglove is well recommended and this can be used comfortably even at odd moments. A chamois leather of generous size is an advantage too. This being used for 'finishing off' with a high gloss effect. Check on the lips, removing any saliva; then clean around the eyes, removing any mucus. The ears should be inspected and cleaned around with a wad of cotton wool. Inspect under the tail and ensure that this area is quite clean too. The proper Boxer needs no trimming, which is another advantage credited to the breed.

## Fighting

The Boxer is not an aggressive dog. He does not look for trouble, but if it is forced upon him he knows how to take care of it, in just the same way as he knows how to select friend from foe. Boxers learn to love their family circle and most will willingly die in defence of master and property. However, sometimes even the best humoured dog is sorely tried in his patience. He might be out with his master, enjoying a peaceful walk in the park when attacked by some unruly canine. It is little wonder that he retaliates and then comes the job of separating them.

With strong dogs this is sometimes far from easy, but when one remembers that in most cases it is usual (although not invariable) for only one to have a hold, the task becomes easier for a single person, although better if two are available. The loose dog (the one which has no hold) should be raised from the ground so that he cannot push in with his hindquarters. The biting dog's loins should then be trapped between the knees of the second person, who should slide his right hand knuckles down underneath the collar, grab and twist the leather, all the time bringing pressure to bear on the biter's windpipe with the other hand.

This position may require to be held for a few moments when the dog with the hold will need to inhale, whereupon their will be a split second of relaxation in the bite. At this point, he can be dragged off, although it is wise to watch now that the loose dog does not seize the hands or rush at his late adversary once he has been freed.

Again, the advisability of thin, strap-type collars being on Boxers during the day, is stressed. Without such a collar it would be virtually impossible to choke off, for the Boxer in action fills out his neck and body steel hard with muscle – a hereditament from the days when as a fighting dog he used this natural 'armour-plate' for protection.

## Elementary training in obedience work

It is never too early to commence training a Boxer. At eight weeks of age a lot of sense exists in that unique headpiece. The average puppy wants to please his owner and will strive hard to understand what is wanted and do it! The master will get greater pleasure by owning such a dog and the dog himself will enjoy life better because he knows he has pleased his master. This is as it should be – understanding and happy accord between master and dog. Training with a small puppy must be of the gradual kind. A puppy inflicted with over-training becomes stale and bored with it all; such a youngster seldom becomes a successful pupil. Not more than ten minutes at a time should be spent in training puppies. At all times he must be treated kindly, intelligently and with commonsense. The occasional titbit reward for good results is essential and this should be accompanied with a pat on the head and a few words of praise.

The following exercises are essential for the welfare of the pet and companion Boxer, making him a welcome member of the family circle, knowing how to behave and becoming unobtrusive when required by his master. If he shows exceptional prowess at the work, then he might even be considered for advanced courses which would allow him to enter Obedience Tests held by some canine societies in conjunction with their own events. There are also registered Training Clubs which hold Obedience Dog Shows and although such bodies aim at standards demanding high canine intelligence, there is no reason why the Boxer cannot achieve top honours in this fascinating pursuit.

'COME' WHEN CALLED

This is a lesson which a dog *must* learn. Any Boxer who does no know when to come when called is an embarrassment, even a liability to his owner as well as being an unhappy dog in the bargain. It is always best to start a training session with the pupil hungry. He will then be more appreciative of the titbit reward which can be won for achievement.

The lesson can be arranged either with one tutor, or two. It is probably quicker taught and more effective with two. Let one person hold the youngster and the other at say ten yards distance call it by name, gently adding 'Come!' The puppy will probably move at once to the caller who should praise him, pat him and award a tasty titbit. This move should then be followed by the same procedure from the helper calling 'Come!' When the puppy has gone away at the second call, he will get another word of praise, another titbit for his good work.

This formula repeated a dozen or more times from one person to the other and back again will sink into his consciousness. It should then be tried by one of the instructors when the puppy is half way back to the other. He should call 'Come!' and if the puppy turns around in his tracks and returns then the praise should be lavish and the titbit an extra good one. Should he not track back but continue to the other person, then he must not be rewarded or praised. Perhaps confused initially, he will soon learn after a few more examples. It is best to give at *least* a dozen lessons to each movement, and to repeat for three consecutive days allowing ample time for the lesson to be learnt.

It is normal to give initial instruction in the precincts of the home and kennel. Not so many distractions exist here as out of doors, so the puppy will learn quicker. However, it is more important for the training to have good effect away from the youngster's usual haunts and as soon as he seems to be ready for the final phase of this lesson he should be taken to a local park or field. Tie a training cord, which can be twenty feet long, to his collar and hold the other end. Release him and puppylike he will at once make a bee-line for some interesting object – a tree, a lake, another dog. As he nears the end of the now running cord which you hold, call 'Come'!

It is likely in his excitement he will be quite heedless of the command and run on, only to be turned head over heels when the cord reaches its extremity! This sudden upset will prove an unpleasant surprise, but it will make him think. After it has been repeated a few times he will halt in his tracks as soon as he hears you call 'Come!' Soon, remembering his starting lesson with this command, he will turn around and walk back to you. This will be the lesson learnt and following a few more tests to ensure that it has 'sunk in', the next simple lesson can be started.

'SIT'

With official obedience training in mind, a dog should be taught always to sit on the handler's left side, hard by the handler's heels when he halts. The dog should be walked on a slack lead, his body close by the handler's left leg. A titbit held in the hand will keep his attention rapt and he will not pull away or be distracted. With the command 'Sit!' the handler should halt suddenly in his tracks, at the same instant swinging his body round to the left without moving his feet. As you do this, the dog should automatically sit. If he carries on walking, snap the lead back firmly from your stationary position, making the dog sit back on his haunches. When he does this, whether naturally or forced by the snap-back method, he should be praised and patted. This will encourage him to do it again. If difficulty is experienced in achieving a sitting position, the dog can be persuaded by taking the collar in the right hand, pulling him back a little and at the same time (with the left hand) pat him down into a sit. If it is found that when he learns to sit on command he sits rather wide of your left leg you might feel inclined to move towards him. This is wrong, you should move away from him even more, then encourage him to narrow the gap with your left hand and some cajolery.

'DOWN'

This exercise can be usefully employed as a 'Part 2' of the 'Sit' routine. Thus, when you have the dog fully taught to obey that command it is already half-way to the completion of the 'Down' lesson! The best method, is again with the pupil on the trainer's left side and the lead under his left foot, its ends held in his right hand. As the command 'Down' is given in a firm tone, the lead is pulled with the right hand; this will cause the dog to be pressed down from the neck end, while with your left hand you press down on his rear section.

'STAY'

This is an important exercise and for simplicity in training it is best to let the exercise follow the mastery of the 'Down' position, as this is the most relaxed attitude the pupil can be in if he is to remain in one spot for an extended period. Having given the command 'Down' and being obeyed, the trainer should now stand in front of him – you can point to the spot where he had downed, if you wish – to emphasize the command 'Stay', as you move back one step. If the dog is restless and gets up to follow you, get him immediately into the 'Down' position. Try again and eventually he will understand that he has to remain there even with a number of yards between you. It is best to make the initial practice still holding his lead. This will allow you a few test steps back; a check cord can play for safety over a longer distance. Soon you will be able to disappear from the dog's view while he remains in the 'Stay' position.

'HEEL'

This is really basic lead training, which has already been covered in the appropriate section. However, it should be remembered that the command 'Heel' is a useful one and one which appears readily understood by the dog. With the dog on the trainer's left side, the lead held in his right hand, a slack loop should be maintained under the dog's neck; in effect, there should be no tautness or tension in the lead. Dog and trainer should start off together with the command 'Heel'. The speed of movement should be gauged so that the lead remains slack and the dog is hard by the trainer's heel at all times. Give the pupil plenty of praise for good results and an occasional titbit. Later, when he is adept, he can be tried without the confinement of the lead. This is the 'heel free' exercise. If he does not appear ready for this at first attempt he should be put back on the lead and given further basic training.

POINTS TO REMEMBER

It is important that the pupil has complete confidence in the master; for this reason, make sure that the dog is not scolded unnecessarily. A violent show of impatience on your part can set back hours of progress. If you make a mistake with your instruction, put it right at once and if the dog seems confused make a fuss of him. If the dog fails to perform satisfactorily in an exercise which he has done previously with perfection, do not let him get away with it. Get him back to the task at once and you will probably find he will do it perfectly. Dogs are quick to take advantage if offered and any slackness condoned while training can delay progress. Watch always for individual reactions in pupils. A method used to train one might well prove totally unsuited to another. If this should be noted then never use it if the pupil finds it unpleasant or fails to learn from its application.

## Training for show

The first thing a show dog must learn is to be handled. This entails standing still while the judge goes over him from nose to tail, feeling, pushing, prodding and shifting all the time. This is how the judge will learn the extent of his development, his structure and his soundness. He must get used to having his lips lifted for examination of the teeth; his private parts handled to ensure that he is entire and his forefeet lifted for feet inspection. A lot of dogs object to such things and those who do seldom get far in the show awards, for the judge quite rightly concurs that a dog who cannot be handled and assessed, cannot be judged.

It is advisable therefore, that when a promising puppy is about to try his luck in the show ring that he should make his debut fully trained in this performance and how to accept it. A good plan is to go through the typical actions of a judge with him at every opportunity. Ask your friends to do the same when they visit you. Strangers too should be invited to run their hands over him to get him used to the routine. A lucky owner is he who owns a good puppy which proves to be a 'natural' showman. This is a dog which does not seem to care how roughly he is pummelled by a judge and enjoys every minute of the show, acts in an orderly fashion and even seems to preen when being exhibited! Given a dog like this there is no need to worry and half the battle is won, but most dogs can, with patience, be trained to perform well, and a good show prospect is worth a few hours training every week.

The best time to start a puppy on his show training course is just before his meal. The best place to do it is somewhere quiet, away from distractions in a spare room or in the garden. If he has had already some of the elementary obedience training discussed he will have learnt the pleasures of doing what he is told and have a good, solid groundwork to offer for this new phase of instruction. He should be on his lead at all times during this course, just as he would be in the show ring. Try him standing to see if he has a *natural* stance, without human assistance. Occasionally, a dog has this and it is preferable to a position into which he has been encouraged by manual placing. If he is structurally sound and typical, it is likely that he will be able to 'show himself', that is, fall into a pleasing and attractive pose. However, if he needs placing by hand, make sure the way you put him is correct and that it displays his good points to advantage while minimising the faults.

Care should be taken not to spread him out too wide in front. The Boxer's legs should be straight and parallel with each other. If you put the palm of your right hand between his legs and under the chest, then lift him slightly off the ground, allowing him to regain the floor naturally, then the right position will be obtained. Check on the forelegs when viewed from the side. They should run vertically from shoulders to ground. The front feet should be parallel with the rear feet too and to example the feet position better each foot should appear in the four corners of an imaginary rectangle when viewed from above. Note however, that Boxer hind stance is unique in that its angulation requires well curved stifles. The hind feet must not therefore, be allowed in a position too far forward or too much under the dog. A study should be made of successful show winners and good Boxer photographs to determine this point and when assessed properly, then emulated.

As soon as the required position has been found and the dog placed in it the command 'Stand' should be given. Every time the dog is put down into place this command should be repeated. No doubt he will fidget at first, but with encouragement and the occasional titbit for co-operative behaviour he will soon learn to stay 'put' and eventually stand firm in his position even when handled. A danger exists with manual placing of this kind, that the exhibit will appear 'wooden'. He need not if his attention is maintained and livened with the anticipation of a titbit from his owner's hand. In any case when he gets to the show ring there will be plenty of interesting dogs and objects to attract him and keep him on his toes.

A puppy being trained in this way should not have more than ten minutes lesson at a time. Youngsters get bored quickly and soon go stale with instruction. This has to be avoided or progress will be retarded. The time is now ripe for the puppy to show how well he can stand with distractions around him. Up to now he has done very well in some quiet nook, but he will find the show ring a very noisy and bustly place with more dogs together than he has ever seen before quite apart from people! He must be taken therefore, to a room or place where many distractions exist. A good idea is to join the local dog-training club. Most of these bodies have their weekly meetings in nearby halls and cost little to join.

Here, the puppy can be taken and get not only the dog show atmosphere he needs to prepare him for his debut at a real show, but expect advice and prompting in the important matters of deportment and posing. Here too, you will be able to deploy him around a ring or up and down so that he gets used to moving a typical distance away from the judge, then turning about face and retracing his steps – just as he would have to do were he being exhibited. An effective way of doing this is to train the dog to turn about face immediately the handler snaps his fingers and a smart turn is achieved thereby. All that has to be done is to snap the fingers as the dog is turned about face, initially by using a drag of the leash. After a few tries he will turn as soon as he hears the snap, no leash pressure being needed.

The pupil must be taught to move at a speed which suits him. At this correct speed he will show his good points to advantage while minimising the effect of his faults. A dog moved too fast or too slow will almost certainly achieve the opposite effect. The proper Boxer gait is bold in its stride, head held high and with alert expression. It stands to reason that if he is pulling or scrambling on his lead that his head will be thrust forward, the shoulders thrown out sideways and his fore-action rendered impossible to assess. Alternatively, if he moves sluggishly, the beautiful and rhythmic muscular co-ordination we expect from the hindparts of a moving Boxer is lost. Teach the dog to make the best of himself at all times; it is just as important too that you remain aware of his good ring behaviour from the moment you enter the ring with him to the time you leave. If you relax for just one second – this might be the very moment when the judge turns on his heel to consider the dog for a placing! If your exhibit looks jaded and is sitting on his haunches instead of looking alert and up on his toes, then he doesn't deserve the prize he might have got! Ringcraft is an exhibitor's science. It needs to be studied with care and applied with skill. Others might have dogs as good as yours, but with your extra knowledge of this way to make the best of a Boxer your chances of beating them are enhanced.

## The kennels

One Boxer is better kept in the house. He will thrive better in the family circle and because he learns quickly to love his people and home he will usually make a better guard. A dog kept out of doors is not much use to anyone. He becomes bored, often lacks affinity with his owner and is quite capable of ignoring any intruder. Some times a Boxer takes time to develop his instincts as a guard dog. An owner should not be too impatient for the dog will soon learn to give warning barks when necessary. Again, a dog kept out of doors alone suffers in the development of his intelligence, whereas the indoor dog seems to know everything which is said to him! However, when a number of dogs are kept, the situation is different. Kennel life becomes essential and there are many comfortable models in pre-fabricated kennels to be bought these days from mail order and local sources.

Great care must be taken to pick the right site for the structure and to ensure it will prove comfortable and allow strict hygiene. The kennel site should not be erected under trees, although a screen of trees protecting it from the prevailing winds of the locality is often to be desired. It should stand on well-drained sandy soil or gravel, preferable facing south or south-west. A range of four adjoining kennels is a nice start for the novice, with a compartment at one end to house brushes, shovel, sawdust and disinfectant supplies with easy access. A further single kennel should be placed well away from the rest to be used as a sick bay in emergency.

Many kennels are insufficiently high. This means that the breeder has to spend his time in them in a hunched-up position, which is neither good for the back nor conducive to good kennel efficiency. It is best to allow at least six feet from floor to roof so people can stand inside with some comfort. Each resident Boxer should have a floor area of about sixteen square feet, at least. If the kennel is to be heated then allow him as much room as possible. With no heating installed, then too much individual space is not such a good thing in winter for the Boxer will be hard put to it to radiate enough body warmth to keep himself cosy. There should be a run of at least eight feet long to every kennel, bounded on both sides and front by a ten feet high chain link fence.

Some Boxers are super jumpers, so to avoid accidents it will be best if the run can be topped with a chain-link or perspex roof. The do-it-yourself kennel builder will be able to produce a lot of refinements and ideas to fit his particular needs, no doubt, but he will be well advised to study a few professional designs before embarking on his own structure. Draught is a known killer and care must be taken that it cannot penetrate the kennel. The sleeping benches should be made to slide out for easy cleaning and it is a good idea to improvise a ventilation system which can be adjusted to suit outside weather conditions.

Always try, if finance permits, to construct doors from the run into the outside world on the 'inner chamber' system. This means two doors in use – the outside one you open to enter then close it with yourself inside. You then open the second door to enter the actual run, safe in the knowledge that the inmate cannot slip past you and escape. Kennel hygiene is vital and this should receive daily attention, going into every corner with a mild disinfectant, a stronger solution being used to swab down the outside concrete runs. 'Dettol' is a well-tried and recommended antiseptic germicide and it can be used for bathing cuts, bites, abrasions and stings too.

## Other lessons

CAR TRAVEL

Always get a dog used to car travel or public transport right from puppyhood. Once he has had all his innoculations he can be taken out in a car either before his meal or at least two hours after it, the reason for this being that he is not so easily induced to actual sickness. With a full stomach before a journey a dog will suffer nausea and either slobber or vomit within a short time of starting off. It is usually those dogs who have been sick in a car who *think* they are going to be sick every time they enter a vehicle thereafter! Providing the puppy can have a few consecutive trips without being sick he is unlikely to experience nausea in future outings.

It is important therefore, to try to avoid sickness on his first car journey. The best way to do this is have a companion with you who will take the puppy on his lap. The first run out should be one of short duration. If the puppy looks uncomfortable and begins to open his jaws spasmodically it is a sign that he feels sick. Stop the car until he has settled down or walk or carry him back home. It will be found that the car trips can be increased in mileage each time out until quite a lengthy trip can be made without the dog feeling ill. By this time there is a good chance that he will have been cured of the weakness.

For chronic cases of car travel sickness there are effective drug remedies on the market which your veterinary surgeon should be asked to prescribe for a Boxer.

NEEDLESS NOISE

The Boxer, in common with others in the Bull Breeds family, is not an unnecessary barker. However, one occasionally encounters a puppy which barks or howls so incessantly as to create a distinct nuisance to owner and neighbours alike. Small puppies cannot understand why they should not make such a noise, so the best method of correction has to be largely psychological. The youngster must be made to learn that every time he opens his mouth to bark or scream something unpleasant happens! When he realises this he will think twice before he starts up again for fear it will trigger off the 'treatment'.

An effective training method is to wait quietly outside the door of the room where he is kept. As soon as he barks without reason, burst open the door and shout 'No!' or 'Quiet!' Taken by surprise he will gape at you and stop barking. Retire at once and again wait outside, waiting for the next bark to come. Almost before it leaves his mouth be in there with the shout of 'No!' or 'Quiet!' The youngster will not like this at all, even less if it is accompanied with a firm tap from a rolled up newspaper! After a few sessions, the puppy will usually give it up as a bad job and retire the loser to his box to muse lugubriously upon the strange ways of humans.

Unless the pupil is quite stupid of course, he will learn quickly not to be so vociferous and it is important that he does, for this habit is a great patience tester. A danger exists of course, in that a puppy which has been trained out of needless barking will not bark a valid warning when required to do so, such as when a fire breaks out or an intruder threatens. However, most Boxers are sensible enough to know when their vocal services are required to guard the home so no worry need ensue on this point.

'JUMPING UP'
Few canine faults annoy so much as the one which makes a dog bound straight out of a muddy garden puddle straight into the lap of a lady guest, ruining her new dress and bespattering all around with filth! Such a dog reflects at once upon his master's aptitude as a trainer and clearly such an irritating habit must be broken. Obviously, the first thing is to ensure at all times that muddy dogs never encounter lady guests, but even the best laid plans go astray and it is as well to prepare some corrective remedy for the next incident.

Patently, the jumper must be pushed quite forcibly away from his target as he leaps. Shout 'Down!' or 'No!' at him loudly, if it is to prove effective for the boisterous dog hears very little when excited and he needs to be halted in his tracks. If the chronic jumper takes little heed of the command, tread on his back paws as you give the command. If this proves fruitless, then bring up one knee and let him bound against that. It will almost certainly topple him over backwards and he will find it most unpleasant. A few lessons like this are calculated to quieten him down and mend his jumping ways.

# 6 Exhibiting

Not many people enter the dog show 'game' of their own volition. They are frequently coerced into making an entry at the local canine society's event by some person, who seeing them with an attractive Boxer, accosts them and informs them the specimen is a good one and 'ought to be shown'. Most owners are quite naturally proud of their pedigree Boxers and it takes very little encouragement, as a rule, to persuade them to try their luck. Knowing next to nothing about the finer points of the breed, let alone the official breed Standard, they hope merely that the dog will win a prize in much the same way as they might buy a raffle ticket. On the other hand, if the dog wins nothing they will not care over much, either. In fact the whole thing is treated like a game – which of course it is at this stage of their interest. Unfortunately, at times, a different aspect arises – their dog, either by virtue of the fact that it has no or only poor competition at the show, wins a major prize. Perhaps other Boxer people present flatter the dog and his owner becomes over-ambitious for him. At times like this, there is a danger that the dog-show 'bug' will bite hard and then maybe the simple recreation of exhibiting becomes less than a pastime, more a business, highly competitive and fraught with rivalry and jealousy.

Let it be said at once that dog showing is a *good* hobby. It is the shop window of the dog world and develops a keen and healthy competitive spirit among its devotees. To some, concerned largely with the commercial potentialities of Boxerdom, it opens up lucrative possibilities for the breed is in demand and produce good prices at home and abroad. Most people who start exhibiting however, are more concerned with getting expert opinion of the judges on their dogs. Later, they will wish to breed from their bitches, hoping always to produce better Boxers in their litters and perhaps be lucky enough to breed a champion. Also, they will strive for premier show awards to improve, even perpetuate their kennel names. Certainly, in the course of their careers they will meet a lot of nice people, make some real and lasting friends and enjoy the social side which exists in dogdom.

**Picking the show**

Both the weekly journals devoted to dogs, viz. *Dog World* and *Our Dogs*, maintain show announcements columns. Here the intending exhibitor will find details of dog shows to be held in the near future. The various types of shows, i.e. Exemption, Sanction, Limited, Open and Championship events will be represented and will offer a good selection for the enthusiast. The procedure is to write or telephone the honorary secretary or show manager of the society concerned and request a schedule of the classification offered. The show might be for Boxers only, in which case it would be termed a Specialist Breed Club event, alternatively, if many different breeds are classified it would be called perhaps an All Breeds or Any Variety event.

Both types of show have their useful features, although it is probably best to enter at shows where only Boxers make the competition. Such a show would be run by one of the specialist societies, a list of whom will be found at the end of this book, and the judge appointed would be a Boxer expert. This means that every Boxer would be judged competently by a specialist and one would possibly get a more detailed opinion of an exhibit from such a person. In any case, both kinds of events should be supported and the Boxer entered under a useful cross-section of all-rounders and specialists in order to test the dog's ability to win in any type of competition.

TYPES OF SHOWS

The Kennel Club licenses a number of different types of dog shows. The most 'junior' form is the Exemption Show. A dog can be entered at such a show even though not registered at The Kennel Club. Neither do the usual Kennel Club Rules apply, except that most of the disciplinary rules have to be observed. For pedigree dogs, only four classes are permitted where they can be judged according to their various breed points and standards. Such classes have to be of a general nature; Any Variety Sporting and Any Variety Open being two examples. It is usual and popular to arrange the remaining classes so that pedigree dogs and mongrels and cross-breeds can compete against each other. These appear as novelty classes such as Dog with the Longest Tail; Dog the Judge would like to Take Home; Dog in Best Condition; Dog with the Most Appealing Eyes and so on. For such shows The Kennel Club does not specify any special entry fee or prize money, neither does it ask for report on the results and awards. Prize cards throughout are white with black printing, unlike the usual show prize cards which have to be red for first, blue for second and yellow for third. Exemption Shows must not be run in conjunction with any registered Canine Society or Training Club, but the officers of such associations may organise or help to run them. Sometimes obedience tests of a simple nature can be incorporated too, but these do not have to be similar to Kennel Club Obedience Tests. Exemption Shows are usually held in aid of charity, often on Bank Holidays.

*Limited Shows.* These are shows held under Kennel Rules and

Regulations, so-called because entry is limited to a certain number of classes and restricted to members of clubs or societies, or to exhibitors within a specified radius or otherwise. Challenge Certificate winners are ineligible at Limited Shows. This type of show is unbenched.

*Sanction Shows*. A Sanction Show is also unbenched. It is confined to members of the club or society which is running the show and no Challenge Certificate winners are eligible. No class higher than Post-Graduate may be classified and only 20 classes are permitted when there are more than one breed or variety. When only one breed such as Boxers is concerned, the show must not comprise more than 10 classes.

*Open Shows*. Such shows can be benched or otherwise. Very often they are held in conjunction with an Agricultural Show events. No restrictions are made as to exhibitors making entries in classes provided; conditions being similar to those at a championship show, but without provision of Challenge Certificates.

*Championship Shows*. These are most important shows and are really Open Shows held under the Rules and Regulations of The Kennel Club at which Challenge Certificates are offered and may be competed for. Some of the all-breed shows can occupy, one, two, even three days; the specialist shows, i.e. shows at which one breed such as Boxers might appear, are one-day events. Cruft's Dog Show, the most important dog show in the world, caters for almost every variety, offering Challenge Certificates for most.

*Matches*. These are not shows in the strict sense of the word, but must not escape mention for they are popular among doggy people. They are conducted under Kennel Club Rules and Regulations, and are competitions on the knock-out system between pairs of dogs, a prize of some description being awarded to the final winner – Best Dog in Match. Clubs run these usually for member-education, either between dogs of club members or in challenge with dogs belonging to members of rival clubs, either with the same breed or different.

It is best to select a show which is reasonably near home and entails therefore, the minimum travel. Later, bigger shows (where better dogs attend and competition is keener), can be supported, and more confidence is gained. However, when the Schedule is received it will be seen that it is laid out with the various classes open to the exhibitor. Whether a dog is eligible for a class can be determined by referring to the printed Definitions of Classes and these, and in fact the entire Schedule, should be studied very carefully until it is understood. With the Schedule will come an Entry Form and this will be found quite simple to complete. Once signed by the owner of the dog to be exhibited it must be returned to the show secretary, postmarked at least not later than the date demanded on the Schedule. An entry posted after closing date for the show would render it invalid and be returned.

## Show preparation

One might own the best Boxer in the land, a veritable paragon of the breed, but if he is not taught to show properly, he will undoubtedly suffer a lot of defeats in the show ring, probably against exhibits of lesser merit than himself, although better trained in the arts of presentation. No judge appreciates or has much patience with the dog who struggles and lunges off when being assessed. In fact, some judges will automatically exclude from the top awards such a foolish creature. A show dog *must* learn to show himself – or better perhaps, let us say that his owner must teach him to perform well to his advantage when in the show ring. It needs a good bit of patience and understanding to achieve prime results with some dogs, but when the Boxer has learnt to pose with effect before the judge, displaying well his best features and obscuring his faults, then the training effort will be deemed worthwhile. It has been explained how some Boxers lend themselves *naturally* to an attractive and effective stance when showing, but such dogs are rare and most have to be taught the art. However good is the dog as a specimen and in his type, he is unlikely to get to the top if poorly trained, against Boxers who excel in ringcraft.

The methods to be employed for training a puppy in deportment in the show ring have been adequately covered in the chapter on general training. It should go without saying that if a dog is to win a prize he must be in first-class condition. This will be revealed by the quality and bloom of his coat, the sparkle and alertness in his eyes and litheness and springiness of his step. The handler himself must contribute to the overall effect by concentrating on the job in hand right from the moment he enters the ring to the time he leaves it after the class has been judged – whether a prize has been won or not. The entire time should be spent in keeping the dog looking good and up on his toes; to slacken off for one moment will be to court disaster, for it is likely that this will be the very second the judge turns on his heel to find his winner! If the favoured one is sitting on his haunches looking bored and wilted at the time, he stands a good chance of being left out of the awards. The exhibitor should always keep a tasty titbit in his pocket – many dogs show better when anticipating one and this is quite legitimate ring procedure.

A Boxer should never, never, be over-handled. Such a specimen often becomes stiff and unnatural in his posture and if called upon by the judge to stand free of his handler invariably presents an unfavourable and wilting aspect. Always get a show dog to 'stand on his own feet'. An exhibit too dependent on his handler seldom goes to the top.

The wise exhibitor will make a number of pre-show tests to ascertain at what speed his Boxer moves best and looks best. This will vary, often quite considerably with individual animals. Unduly slow movement in a Boxer will hardly do justice to his 'natural' gait and will reveal at once to an

Messrs Somerfield and Harvey's Faerdorn Impressionist.

experienced judge's eye any small structural faults which might exist to militate against correct movement. Conversely, action which is unnaturally fast will tend to visually confuse the superb hind locomotion we have come to expect from the sound modern Boxer. Similarly, speeds of action which are too fast or too slow will lessen the impact of the dog's positive front movement which a judge likes to see in a Boxer. The only speed to move a show Boxer at is the speed which suits him – this is the *right* speed and to get this the novice should obtain the assistance of an experienced breeder and exhibitor to determine it as far as his own dog is concerned. The dog should be moved away from, then towards the helper until his eye tells him that at last the correct style of action and effective gait has been achieved. Once this has been resolved, this speed should be practised by *both* parties continually until it becomes virtually automatic to exhibit and exhibitor alike. Assuming that the assessment of speed has been correctly determined, it will be found that the Boxer will display his beautifully muscled hindquarters to maximum advantage and his forward actions will be springy, athletic and indicative of great stamina.

It can happen that a judge will ask the handler to move his dog at a special slow or fast speed in order that he can decide some particular point of judging the dog. Such requests need occasion no resentment in the owner; in fact, all instructions from the judge in the ring should be followed without demur for they are seldom made without some specific purpose in mind.

Mrs F. M. Price's Felcign Servais.

## Show paraphernalia

Most shows are well organised for exhibitor comfort, but it is as well to go to every dog show well prepared. The prudent exhibitor will carry a special case with him and this will contain a variety of things likely to be required. If the show is a benched one, then a bench chain to secure the dog to his compartment is essential. Make sure when it is fixed that it is neither too long (thus allowing him to topple from his bench or engage with the adjacent dog) nor too short to permit reasonable comfort (he should be able to curl up). It is wise to carry a dog blanket too. This can be spread on the bench or even beside the exhibitor's chair, should it be an unbenched show. It does afford some degree of insulation from infection and can be washed any number of times. Do not forget to include a small first-aid kit and bottle of antiseptic, also a brush or hand-glove.

Take a plastic feeding dish and container with milk or water, just in case it is difficult to secure a drink for the dog. If it seems likely that you will be many hours from home a light meal can be packed for the dog, and one's own personal needs must not be overlooked. Important too are titbits for the exhibit and the show passes and ring numbers, if these have been forwarded by post in advance of the show.

Never feed the dog before he enters the ring. In a warm atmosphere particularly, a fed dog quickly becomes sluggish and indifferent to his duties, whereas a hungry one is usually up on his toes, showing interest in his surroundings and especially the provocative titbit. When he has completed his classes he can be fed if required, and allowed a drink. If the dog is benched, make sure he is exercised at intervals, but be cautious of Kennel Club Rule B.1. 19(a) and (b) which forbids a dog's absence from his bench while exercised for longer than fifteen minutes. It is important to recommend at this stage that every exhibitor must acquaint himself with all the Kennel Club Rules and Regulations concerning shows.

## Kennel Club Matters

REGISTERING THE BOXER

All Boxers should be registered at The Kennel Club. In any case, this is essential before a dog is used at stud or a bitch bred from. A form by which application for registration is made is obtainable from The Kennel Club offices, which are 1/4 Clarges Street, Piccadilly, London, W1Y 8AB (Tel: 01-493 6651). This form needs to be signed in the appropriate section by the breeder and further details required are the breed, the date of birth, colour and markings, the sex, also the names and registration numbers of both sire and dam and the names of the grandparents. The same form will show the names and addresses of the owner of the Boxer to be registered and the owner of the dam, the latter person of course being in effect, the breeder.

A selection of from one to four required names can be entered on the form in order of preference. There is no guarantee that The Kennel Club will allow any of the names requested in the application in which case they will suggest a name if you wish it. The detail on the form will be checked and if found correct a Registration Card will be issued, the Boxer's new registration number being shown on the card. The registrations will be published in a subsequent issue of *The Kennel Gazette*.

A dog's initial registered name, including hyphens and apostrophes must not exceed a total of 24 letters.

An exhibition point which concerns some people might be commented upon here. When; at the date of closing of entries for a show, an exhibitor has applied for, but not received, the certificate of registration from The Kennel Club, the dog shall be entered in the name shown as first choice on the application for registration form. This should be followed by the letters 'N.A.F.' (Name Applied For). Observance of this matter will simplify the situation regarding prize awards should the exhibit be placed.

## Selling puppies

ADVERTISING

It is wise to make early plans for disposing of at least some part of the home-bred litter. Boxers grow on quite fast from two weeks of age and by the time they have been completely weaned at say, five weeks of age, they are making their presence felt – to say the least! Some breeders are fortunate in that they have their puppies booked to buyers almost as soon as they are born. Providing these bookings are accompanied with deposits and are not just promises, this is a very happy state of affairs for the breeders.

However, beware the jovial acquaintance who says grandly, that he will have a puppy, but forgets to mention the promise to his wife – who is probably the one who will have to care for it. Such orders are usually cancelled inconveniently just a day or so before the puppy is ready to go and are not worth the words wasted on them. Most breeders have to think about finding the youngsters good homes by the time they are six weeks old. If one or two perhaps, are being retained due to their show promise the sooner a final decision is made on them the better. It is not easy to pick the best from a good uniform litter of say six or seven and if the breeder doubts his ability to decide the best he will be well advised to bring in a few expert friends, give them all a drink and leave it to them. By this method, he should gain enough comment to decide upon a common denominator in the litter, which he can keep for himself as the pick.

Once this has been done, the others should be sent away to their new homes, so they can start their lives independently of their fellows. They will all thrive better on their own once settled in. Most well reared puppies of this breed are prepared for solo existence with a good family by the time they are just over six weeks old. The best media to use for advertising stock for sale, are weekly journals devoted to dogs. One is *Dog World*, the other *Our Dogs*, both obtainable at any news-stand. The puppies should be offered in the Boxer section and in such papers one might reasonably expect to get the best selling prices, unlike local newspapers which seem to attract a clientele less prepared to pay high prices for dogs. In both the above-mentioned papers some indication of the puppies' breeding would be expected and understood by most buyers. For instance, a display advertisement might read:

Famous 'BANDITS' Boxers

offer for sale 3 outstanding dog puppies (2

fawn 1 brindle) ready now. Sire : Ch. Bandits

So-and-So, Dam : Ch. Bandits Whosagirl, the

producer of 3 Cruft's Bests of Breed. KC Regd.

Prices moderate. Write or telephone : Mr......

...............................................................

On the other hand if advertising is confined to the lay press, do not waste lines giving details of the ancestry or brilliant show potential of the stock, for such is completely lost on the average pet buyer likely to answer your advertisement. It is much better therefore, to concentrate on the breed's intelligence, its ability to guard and innate love for children and loyalty – all points calculated to appeal to the layman. Always be honest in an advertisement – never overstate, for this can cause customer resentment later on as well as suspicion. Here is an example of advertising in national or local newspapers:

BOXER PUPPIES. Both sexes ready now. First class pedigree; Kennel Club registered. Ideal as guard for home and children; highly intelligent. Moderate prices Mr............................................
......................................................

THE SELLING

The enquiries received in response to such advertisements should be enough to dispose of the puppies you have to sell. A lot may depend on the time of the year you have them. The months immediately prior to the popular holiday periods are seldom good for puppy sales, whereas January to March and September onwards usually develop well. A lot of people expect to get even pedigree puppies for next to nothing, having not the slightest conception of present-day expenses associated with puppy rearing and stock feeding. It is best to fix a price in advance of people calling, and once this is done keep to it and do not countenance haggling.

It is relatively simple to ascertain the current market price of a Boxer puppy and if a ready sale is wanted, then the litter can be made available at favourable terms. Some breeders graduate their prices according to their assessment of the value of the individual; thus they will tell a customer that puppies are for sale from a certain price. However, the best way to sell is to make a standard price for each puppy, unless there is a runt or poorly coloured one which will have to be sold at a very much lower price; or even a 'flyer' which on the other hand, might prove worth a few pounds more. If a customer insists on making his own selection from the litter, there is nothing against allowing this privilege, providing he is one of the early visitors to the kennel while the litter is intact. Frankly, it is better to produce only *one* puppy for each and every enquiry. Not many people coming to purchase a puppy know what to look for. One puppy put before a customer delights him and he buys it; two puppies confuse him and he ponders over-long, the entire litter at his feet frequently sends him away a non-buyer. Should he make a selection he is unlikely to feel confident that he has chosen the right one and he seldom goes home as happy as the man who has a puppy selected for him by the breeder.

Some Boxer kennels will buy entire litters of well-bred and sound puppies, especially if the puppies have been sired by one of their stud dogs. Naturally, they pay rather less than the breeder would get were he to sell his puppies individually, but it frequently proves economical in the long run. This is because the puppies will be off his hands by the time they are six weeks of age as a rule. Likewise, the responsibility of advertising, selling, despatch and after-sales service, etc., all factors liable to harass the small private breeder, is taken over by the kennel.

Always take a deposit, to show good faith, from each person who books a puppy. Never hand over or send away a puppy unless the full purchase price is in hand first. Some people are very slow at paying once they have possession.

If you are prepared to keep a puppy for two or three weeks after it has been sold to oblige a buyer who is unable to accommodate it at once, get the full purchase price first and make sure that the client understands what he will have to pay you per week for the puppy's food and kennelling. Remember to take into account that a small puppy requires a lot of meal times and general attention. Never sell young puppies to homes where undisciplined children abound, for so often they become just playthings, ill-treated and later discarded when their novelty has worn thin. Such dogs live miserable lives, neither do they give pleasure to their owners, through no fault of their own. Always try and determine what is a good home, either by enquiry or by making a personal visit to the client's home if he lives nearby.

EXPORTING

Boxers have always been popular abroad and British breeders find a constant demand for their good stock from overseas enthusiasts. Sending Boxers abroad is a specialised business and unless the private exporter is prepared to go to a great deal of trouble it is far better to entrust the work to one of the several companies well-versed in the technique. Where possible consign by air, it usually proves much cheaper than by surface travel and it is certainly quicker; much better for the animal too.

## Rescue Service

This is a humane service of rehabilitation managed by the Boxer Breed Council. It endeavours to rehouse Boxers who have become destitute for diverse reasons. Most breeds, these days, have their Rescue Officers spread nationwide and the Boxer Rescue Scheme has its honorary workers in most counties of the UK. Their task is not always an enviable one. Dogs come before them in varying states due to dumping (which is becoming increasingly prevalent) or to poor upbringing with bad environmental background history and such as these often create heartbreaking problems requiring serious decisions.

RESCUE UNITS AFFILIATED TO BOXER BREED CLUBS
*Secretary Boxer Breed Council* and able to give names/addresses of all Boxer Rescue contacts:
Miss Ann M. Podmore, Farthing Ridge, 89A High Street South, Stewkley, Leighton Buzzard, Beds. LU7 OHU. Tel: 052 524 288

*Midland Boxer Club*
Mrs Peggie Ingram, Bockendon Kennels, Cromwell Lane, Tile Hill, Coventry. Tel: 0203 466706
Mrs Margaret Buck, 8 Dugard Place, Barford, Warwick. Tel: 0926 68215
Mrs Pat Withers, Warwick Cottage, Corfton, Craven Arms, Salop. Tel: 058 473 647

Mrs Kay Bradbury, 15 Trafalgar Road, Moseley, Birmingham. Tel. 021 440 2778 (Wkg. Hours)

*Mancunian Boxer Club*
Mrs Doreen Hall, 251 Ainsworth Road, Bury, Lancs. Tel: 061 764 5593

*Merseyside Boxer Club*
Mrs Marjorie Burnett, 640 Leyland Lane, Leyland, Lancs. Tel. 0772 421946
Mrs V. Grant, 93 Park Road, Meols, Hoylake, Wirral. Tel: 051 632 5852
Mrs J. Buckley, Bow Stone Gate, Disley, Nr Stockport. Tel: 06632 5541

*Northern Boxer Club*
Mrs Slater and Mrs Waring, 28/30 Newlaithe Hill, Newsome, Huddersfield, W. Yorks. Tel: (0484) 533801 or 540604

*South Western Boxer Club*
Mrs J. Mould, Felden Boxers, S. Petherton, Somerset. Tel. 0460 235

*Scottish Boxer Club*
Mrs Rhonda Watson, (Co-ordinator), 29 Greenvale Drive, Brightons, By Falkirk. Tel: 0324 713511. For Scottish Boxer Rescue contact addresses.

*Tyne Wear and Tees Boxer Club*
Mrs J. Ellison, 39 Hulton Avenue, Hartlepool. Tel: 0429 70811
Mrs J. Smith, 7 Ventnor Road, Linthorpe, Middlesborough, Cleveland T55 6DX. Tel: 0642 827295

*Norfolk Boxer Rescue affiliated to Broadlands Boxer Training Club*
Mrs Heather Smith, (Co-ordinator) The Gables, 344 Holt Road, Horsford, Nr Norwich. Tel: 0603 897555
Mrs Sue Huff, Cosy Corner, The Loke, Waterloo Road, Hainford, Norwich. Tel: 0603 897463
Mr R. Cook, 76 Falcon Road West, Sprowston, Norwich. Tel: 0603 46093

*Boxer Rescue – Southern Unit*
Mr Les Crawley, 37 Highview Way, Patcham, Brighton, Sussex. Tel: 0273 505770

*Cotswold Boxer Rescue*
Mrs Pat Banks, 23 Cashes Green Road, Cainscross, Stroud, Gloucestershire. Tel: 045 36 5251

*North Wales*
Mrs E. Shields, 1 Hillside Cottages, Dolgarrog, Conway. Tel: 049 269 265

*Devon and Cornwall*
Mrs Dorothy Muzzelle, Leburnick Boarding Knls., Lawhitton, Launceston, Cornwall. Tel: 0566 2635

*Hampshire/Dorset*
Mrs Jean Scheja, Appletree Cottage, Lower Common Lane, Three Legged Cross, Wimborne. Tel: 0202 822496

*Cheshire*
Mrs S. Jones, 15 Church Street, Davenham, Northwich. Tel: 0606 3504

# 7 Judging the Boxer

The Boxer breed is one fortunately rich in competent judges, not only in the United States of America, but in Britain and on the Continent of Europe. Breeds so well endowed progress well and establish better in the field of pedigree dogs. The poor judge and the corrupt one do a disservice not only to the exhibitors who enter before them, but to the breed as a whole.

Every judge should have a clear understanding of the Boxer breed Standard, for this is the standard of perfection in the breed, and although it is reasonably certain that the perfect Boxer has yet to be born, at least the judge should have him pictured mentally. Not only this, but it would seem reasonable to demand that at some time or other he should have owned or regularly handled a good one himself. He will need a lengthy period of experience in Boxers behind him and he should be a constant visitor to shows where Boxers are classified. In effect, he should be well steeped in Boxerdom before he has the temerity to accept a judging appointment. His training will enable him to absorb the best features from every good Boxer he sees and handles. When he enters the ring to judge his mind should have fixed a picture of not the best Boxer there is, but the best Boxer imaginable.

Judging is largely a matter of comparison, dog for dog. Proportion, breed type and soundness are the primary considerations and a dog must be judged not in his respective lack of faults, but certainly according to his *good* points, which means that judging should be on positive rather than negative features. The judge should have an honest, open mind and avoid at all costs exaggeration in fanciers' points and seek bone, balance and substance, soundness and Boxer character. He should assess his dogs from front, rear and both sides. Good movement is essential, a Boxer with excellent action is usually a sound one, conversely not many dogs move well if unsound structurally. He will have learned that a dog moved slowly will more often display weaknesses in its make-up than one exhibited at a canter. He will know that sometimes good presentation on the part of the exhibitor, good showmanship by the dog and a flashy marking can deceive and be mistaken for quality. Such things he will guard against when judging. Also, he will look for correct breed type. Type, as we have said, is difficult to define, but broadly speaking breed type depends largely on the dog's anatomical structure and general appearance, whereas individual type is expressed more by points and detail. He will know how much easier it is to judge a class of good ones than an entry of mediocre and poor ones and he will instinctively ferret out the fault which the occasional exhibitor will endeavour to hide from him by strategic handling.

A judge must learn to rely entirely upon himself in the ring. The stewards may be good and reliable but they must not be depended upon. One well-known British judge refused to accept steward help – in fact, after each class had been judged he preferred to have the next class with its 'seen' dogs and 'unseen' dogs all jumbled up together! He never reversed a decision or faltered in his placings either and made a big impression on dogdom thereby. He was either an exceptionally self-assured judge or he had a remarkable memory! Nevertheless, this is as it should be when judging and a good judge should be able to make his placings at any time and justify his reasons for so doing.

INSIDE THE RING

As the exhibitors and their dogs enter the ring for the class to be judged, the experienced judge will stand at one end of the arena and watch them. Some will look good, some mediocre, others will seem perhaps third and fourth raters. This initial casting of the eye over exhibits often proves useful to a judge in separating mentally the gold from the dross among his exhibits, but it is a system which seldom proves entirely conclusive. Too often, a dog which looks quite sensational as he enters the ring, will on examination be found lacking in several essential features; whereas an average looking Boxer at first glance, later evinces characteristics which brand him as winning material.

Sometimes a dog's markings are unfortunate. One with a spiral of white from the foot to above the pastern might seem to be light in bone or lacking musculation. A splash of white on the front so placed to optically delude against proper depth of chest are just two possible illusions the pre-meditating judge might experience; proving the inadvisability of judging a dog before handling him. Every exhibit should be afforded enough time for a complete overhaul. The exhibitor having paid his entry fee is entitled to this, at least. Too many judges give but cursory checks on the dogs, either because they are blasé or do not know their job. This attitude does not help Boxer entries at future shows and a lot of exhibitors depart disgruntled and disheartened with the game.

The exhibits should be called over to the judge one by one from their positions around the inside of the ring. The exhibitor who is first in line will pose his dog a few paces before the judge, who will advance and inspect it, taking first its head in his hands and exploring the contours of the skull, the width between the ears and these appendages too. This is what he should find:

HEAD: This is the major component of the Boxer's physical make-up. It has

Mrs J. Royle's
Onstage Fiasco.

to be *clean* in its contour. This means that the outline or general effect of the head is not marred with excess wrinkle. Wrinkles can be expected on top of the skull when the dog is alert and folds are always evident from the root of the nose running downwards on both sides of the muzzle. Overweight of wrinkle in the permitted places or where it should never appear will make a Boxer's head look alien. A Bulldog aspect indicates reversion to an early type of ancestor, which is obviously incorrect. A head devoid of wrinkle on the other hand would look so plain as to detract completely from all that is desired in the breed, such a head being usually of Great Dane stamp.

The head when viewed in profile should reveal a muzzle length which is to the length of the head from the top of the skull to the nose tip as 1 is to 3. It is in this viewing position that most can be learnt about the head and comparative judging simplified. The stop, which might as well be named the 'step', so suggestive is it as a step from muzzle to brow in the Boxer head profile, must be deep and distinct. Lack of stop is a bad fault, as is a muzzle which is frequently found too light and small to properly balance the head.

The determining factor in a good *overall* head study is correct muzzle, for on this depends typical Boxer expression. Without a muzzle of considerable width and depth this cannot be entirely achieved; the lighter and weaker becoming the muzzle the more will expression suffer. 'Harmonious Proportion' is a likely phrase and a good one to insist on when assessing a Boxer's head and muzzle relationship. The cheeks should never bump with muscle; it being required that they should blend nicely with the muzzle to get the Boxer's noble aspect which is probably best seen from a frontal view. Dogs with heavy cheek muscles look too Bull-doggy and frequently carry muzzles which are concertina-ed into the head, showing an unpleasant marked turn-up which often reveals teeth and sometimes tongue. Such are bad faults and must be penalised when judging. The nose tip should rise *slightly* higher in plane from the point where the muzzle roots into the front of the skull. Correctly featured, this contributes to Boxer type; over-done it becomes distinctly 'dish-faced'; therefore a fault.

EYES: These contribute largely towards the requirements of energy and intelligence. Their size, shape, colour and emplacement have to be right, for all are ingredients towards perfection. The eyes of the Boxer tell a good deal about his character and health. They should be dark brown with an amiable, intelligent, somewhat fulgent expression. It should be an 'honest' outlook, but clearly alert and comprehending. Some relation to coat colour can be conceded, providing this is not allowed to go too far into the extremes, especially towards exceptional lightness which apart from going against what the Standard demands can give an impression of shrewdness, as opposed to intelligence, the former being quite alien to the breed. The bulbous or protruding eye is a vulnerable one unsuited to a 'working' breed. Its converse, the small, deep set eye gives an alien expression, often glinting and mean, especially when set too close together. Loose eyelids showing haw is most objectionable in the breed and can prove a nuisance to the Boxer himself for they can collect dust, grit or pollen, causing intense irritation.

EARS: These too must contribute to the ideal Boxer expression. They need to be set at the highest points on the side of the skull, lying flat and close to the cheek when in repose. Big ears detract at once from the proper Boxer appearance; the most important factor is that they should be *tidy* and well controlled and fairly thin in texture.

MOUTH: Some degree of projection in the lower jaw is natural to the Boxer, but when in excess it becomes objectionable, for it is then accompanied by sight of the teeth and tongue. The main thing is that the 'bite' should be serviceable, with a lower jaw formation such that the canines are well separated and the incisors in a straight line giving good width across. In fact, the correct formation of the muzzle depends on ample width here coupled with good width across the upper jaw incisors which should be slightly concave (as viewed from *inside* the dog's mouth, of course!) and fitting comfortably and normally inside the upper row of teeth. The lips contribute a lot to muzzle formation. The upper lip, being tissued generously pads out the space between upper and lower dentition, its lower edges resting comfortably on the upper edges of the bottom lip. It should be noted at this point that the repandus or bent upward part of the lower jaw should bend out but not rise above the front of the upper lip, neither should it disappear beneath it.

NECK: This part of the Boxer's anatomy is made up with seven vertebrae of the spine running from the head to the beginning of the backbone. It contributes to Boxer elegance and nobility of his head carriage, for a good head should have a powerfully muscled neck to support and administer it. However, on the other hand, the effect of a good head is nullified if the neck is weak and unable to direct properly its action. A too-short neck lacks striking power and will carry loose skin and dewlap. The neck line which curves too much from occiput to withers should be noted as a bad fault. It frequently appears with specimens sway-backed and shelly. A short neck running too quickly into the shoulders is often accompanied with a top line which slopes and falls away over the croup, both weaknesses.

FOREQUARTERS: The Boxer should have a good straight front. One which is not will immediately render him as a weak, probably unbalanced specimen. There should be no deficiencies such as looseness at the shoulders and elbows or any weakness at the pasterns. The forelegs need to be well spaced to permit ample chest development, and this should be deep, muscular and contributory to the dog's balance. Bone should be ample in its development. The line of front, i.e. that drawn from a point level with the dog's underjaw down past his shoulders, elbows, forearms to feet, should be refined and indicative of long-muscled grace and strength. Watch will be kept for development which is too narrow or coarse. Tight shoulders militate against proper gait; straight ones produce a 'proppy' movement or mincing action which is most untypical.

BODY: The Standard is fully descriptive of the body properties to seek in the Boxer. It must be muscular and hard and immensely powerful in a medium sized framework. In spite of the strength therein, it must possess quality and grace. Being a dog requiring much stamina, the rib-cage must be big to allow plenty of heart room and to support the respiratory machinery which would be severely taxed in action. The deep chest should be just visible in front of the forelegs when the dog is viewed in profile and the lower line of the chest is at its best development when it passes just through the point of elbow. The body should carry no surplus fat, especially at the loins. The topline should be level and the dog well coupled, i.e. his parts nicely fused together. The swayback, shown by a dip behind the shoulders and the roach back, shown in a convex back-line are inherent weaknesses and consequently bad faults.

HINDQUARTERS: These should be hard muscled yet resilient and well-toned. This section of the dog contains much of his beauty and elegance, especially in action for he is propelled by this sound machinery. The formation of the Boxer hindquarters is important therefore, and providing it is supported with correct angulation of the skeleton it is capable of allowing the dog to travel and work long distances. The proportion of hock to ground as to hip to ground should be as 1 is to 3, in correct construction, this being accompanied by a well-bent stifle. The legs should be parallel when viewed from behind allowing ample room for direct stride and great thrust, with dynamic power. This means that each and every part of this propelling machinery needs to be well-oiled and moulded into an efficient whole. The efficient judge will observe especially second thigh and stifle development of the exhibit. Over-straight stifles are frequently weak in the patella area, lameness occurring without warning. Too much heavy muscle on the posterior is unsightly in a breed which requires refined musculation as opposed to coarse development, liable to fatty degeneration. Faults such as cow-hocks (points of hocks turning in to each other); in-toes (points of hocks turning away from each other with the result that the toes of hind feet turn in) will render an exhibit totally unable to evince good movement. An unsightly fault is sometimes found in Boxers – this is a croup which slopes off excessively. The fault is not as common as it used to be, but it needs constant attention in the breeding field, in order that it can be eradicated. A Boxer so afflicted must have faulty movement because the joint ligaments in his hindquarters have become extended beyond normal.

FEET: Some judges appear to put these well down the line in items of importance, whereas, they should be well to the fore. A Boxer depends on his feet to withstand his efforts over long distances and to be springy and muscular enough to control his movements from a standing position. The Standard asks for a foot which is tightly arched and muscular like a cat's foot. Some think that possibly a foot slightly less bunched-up than a feline's would have suited the Boxer better, but nevertheless the breed foot needs to be strong and well-formed and the pastern, when viewed from the side is better when lying back just a couple of degrees from the true vertical, whereas from the front it should be straight in line with the foot. Feet with open digits are weak; those which are flat and open are weaker. Such feet are frequently inherited, but many can be improved with rough-ground exercising, also Calcium-D sprinkled over the dog's food. The judge will fault feet which are turned out or turned in (pin-toes) as both will interfere with gait, stance and working ability.

TAIL: A reasonably well set tail usually indicates a high croup. When a Boxer is roach-backed, his croup slopes too much and the set-on of tail is too deep. This not only spoils his effect when standing and moving, but broadcasts the fault. Any judge will spot the signal.

COAT: The Boxer coat is short, shiny, smooth and worn tight to the body. It will gloss well and good bloom usually means good condition and full health in the owner. It moults a little, but seldom constitutes any annoyance in the home. The two major colour descriptions in the breed 'Fawn' and 'Brindle' each have their numerous shades. Naturally, some judges have preference for one or the other, but this inclination should not be expressed when making awards. So long as the colour is a permitted one by the breed Standard, the quality of the exhibit must come first, although even in some disciplined adjudicators there exists a leaning towards those handsome red-fawns which sport the popular dark mask and stylish well-placed white blaze. The judge will insist on seeing a black nose. Very often specimens which abound with white on the muzzle surface carry a butterfly nose (flesh patches on the black pigment). Eventually, the flesh sections will disperse and the nose usually blackens over completely. If it fails to, the specimen will fail as a show dog. All white specimens are not accepted in the show ring, although many breeders produce them from the leading bloodlines. They are either destroyed at birth or sold as pets without pedigree. No Boxer is likely to achieve success if his white markings exceed more than one-third of his coat area. Such a coat is termed a 'check' and, as one entirely white, is treated as seriously defective. In conclusion, it should be noted that the dark mask is essential and when white appears on the muzzle of a Boxer its outline should never obscure this handsome adornment.

WEIGHT AND SIZE: As most of the dogs being exhibited will be of 'average' weight and size, as required by the breed Standard, any which fail to conform either by being too large or too small will quickly become apparent! As a breed, the Boxer is termed a medium-sized dog. With proper development, good bone and substance and with these – true balance, which is essential, he will scale in pounds around the middle-sixties and stand at the withers twenty-four inches, these measurements applying to the male, the females being about four pounds and four inches less. Many present-day Boxers come slightly less all round which does not matter too much so long as good type is being standardised within such reasonable limits.

FAULTS: Anyone can fault a Boxer – it is much more difficult to assess and put in order of merit the good points. In judging, too many so-called 'experts' go straight to the exhibit and look for the one or two faults they know they cannot go wrong on. If they find these; even one of them, they have 'faulted' the dog and in their book that means they have damned it. A good judge takes the Boxer as a whole and judges it thus, never separating it into parts and judging them individually. His experience will allow him to mentally grade indifferent appearance and unsound function against such undesirable faults as weak muzzle, light eyes and Terrier-like expression. He will never damn a dog on one fault alone unless he is forced to employ that fault as a deciding factor between two otherwise well-matched exhibits. The faults are all detailed in the Standard for the reader and enthusiast to understand. Faults are easy to find, not so easy to disperse perhaps, but at least open for modification by the determined breeder.

# 8 Diseases, Ailments, Conditions

Not many Boxers go through their lives without experiencing at least some sickness or disease which requires nursing care at home. Clearly, a book of this category is unable to engage professionally in the subject, although the commoner ailments are dealt with to give the inexperienced owner some guidance as to maintaining his dog in good health and to care for him in the most effective way when he is sick. The best investment against illness is of course, good rearing from puppyhood, nutritive feeding and conditioning with ample exercise, intelligent maintenance and control. A good dog is worth all the good things one can put into him, more important, he must be immunised against the serious virus diseases which scourge dogs.

These include Distemper, Hard-Pad, Hepatitis also the bacterial disease known as Leptospirosis, which is contracted from the urine of rats. While Distemper and Hard-Pad are far less menacing than they used to be, due to modern vaccine techniques, they, like the others, need preventive action by the dog owner. This is available in the form of different immunisers, which can be inoculated by the qualified veterinarian. If one resides outside Great Britain it is as well to discuss these safeguards with a qualified authority as sometimes vaccines vary in their form and effect, especially in hot countries.

It has been explained in Chapter Three (Breeding/Hand Rearing) that a puppy within the first twenty-four hours of its life absorbs from its dam's milk flow, a valuable antibiotic substance called Colostrum. This is a natural protection which contains globulin, acting as a mild laxative and casting out impurities collected by the puppy while in its mother's womb. It is believed that Colostrum continues its protective effect for from nine to twelve weeks from birth. Modern veterinary science recommends therefore that artificial protection such as certain injections can offer should be employed as from this stage. It will be realised that a hand-reared puppy, an orphan which has never enjoyed its dam's milk and absorbed Colostrum, will be especially vulnerable to virus and bacterial diseases. Such a puppy will have to be specially immunised in the form of gamma globulin, as soon as the veterinary surgeon advises.

## Infectious and contagious diseases

DISTEMPER

One of the earliest known canine diseases, the dog being most open to it when between the ages of three and eighteen months, although it can be caught anytime. Modern veterinary medicine seems to have mastered its effects which include pneumonia, enteritis symptoms and so on, but the worst part of it in patients seemingly cured is the aftermath of Chorea, etc., nervous disorders which can seldom if ever, be corrected.

The symptoms usually noted with the oncoming of viral infection are loss of appetite, diarrhoea, possibly vomiting and some swelling of the neck glands. The owner should take the patient's temperature and any reading over 102 degrees F should be the signal to get veterinary advice. The dog will want to sleep more than normal, possibly his eyes will become bloodshot and a dry cough will be noted. Feeding should be cut down drastically, boiled water and honey being recommended to allay increased fever. It is not unusual for a sufferer to have little fits, but these should pass with the curing of the disease.

The usual time to have a dog injected with vaccine against Distemper is at three months of age, although some proprietary vaccines are claimed effective at around two months of age. Immunity is reasonably secure, but it is advisable to have 'booster' inoculations at recommended intervals. These will give continued protection.

HARD-PAD

This appears a close relative in the virus field to Distemper, but is a harsher disease and more distressing, also more serious. It is really a form of Encephalitis, consequently it needs immediate treatment, although in its early stages it might be confused with Distemper as the symptoms are similar, and in fact initial treatment is as for that disease. Occasionally, the Hard-Pad victim will become encrusted around the eyes and nostrils and the pads of the feet will swell and harden. The veterinary surgeon will know how to deal with this disease, which can prove fatal.

HEPATITIS

Canine Virus Hepatitis or Rubarth's Disease. Highly infectious, it can prove a speedy killer, although a dog which has managed to survive five days will often pull through. The virus attacks the liver and blood vessels, jaundice being an unpleasant symptom, also a temperature of up to 104°F, with abnormal sleepiness, no appetite, diarrhoea and vomiting. Bitches with this disease have been afterwards affected adversely in their productive powers and the ever increasing incidence of 'fading' puppies has been atttributed to the effect of this disease. The vaccine used is one which acts jointly against the virus with Distemper and Hard-Pad.

LEPTOSPIROSIS

Two forms of this disease are encountered, one being Leptospiral Jaundice (*L. icterrohaemorrhagia*), the other *L. canicola*. The former attacks the liver and is contracted from the urine of rats. This causes jaundice and internal haemorrhage and is obviously very dangerous. The latter attacks the kidneys, the infection coming from the urine of an infected dog. It is the less virulent of the two varieties of bacteria, but although a dog might seemingly be cured after just a few days of fever and depression, it is believed that some damage might affect his kidneys, proving fatal in later life. It is almost impossible for the layman to differentiate between the two forms, diagnosis and specialised treatment being the job of the veterinary surgeon. Vaccination covers both types, a further injection being given after a fortnight. Every effort should be made to eliminate rats in the area if they are suspected and strict hygiene in the kennel is essential, especially as it is thought a dog can be a carrier for the disease through his urine for some time after being cured.

While on the subject of diseases which attack the dog, mention should be made of two more which might be encountered.

COCCIDIOSIS

This is a highly infectious disease requiring strict kennel hygiene as it is contracted from stools, in which the spore forms of the parasite exist. The parasite itself is not unlike the one which attacks poultry and the affected dog will sicken and lose weight quickly. Blood-spattered diarrhoea is a typical symptom and this bowel disorder needs early correction by taking the dog off raw meat and concentrating on milky feeds meanwhile.

PARVOVIRUS ENTERITIS

A comparatively 'new' disease to dogs is Parvovirus. It was unknown before 1978 and it has been responsible for high mortality in many breeds. It is similar to Feline Enteritis and its symptom is severe and frequently fatal gastro-enteritis in the dog, usually affecting puppies just out of the weaning stage. Older dogs are sometimes affected and the disease is unusual in that it reaches the intestine by way of the circulatory system instead of passing through the alimentary tract. The faeces are frequently blood-stained and an infected dog could pass on the disease by its excretions. Temperatures can be either normal or sub-normal; heart failure is not uncommon, caused by damage to the dog's heart muscle.

Immediate veterinary attention is called for when the disease is suspected. Incubation period is 5 + days, infected animals vomiting followed by diarrhoea. Veterinary treatment will include fluid therapy and antibiotics. An excellent vaccine is in use which will allow a high level of protection. It is given initially at 15 weeks of age although some practitioners suggest it at 6 weeks and again at 15 weeks. Boosters follow annually. Its success is being well monitored.

TETANUS

This is contracted through open wounds. Known as 'Lockjaw', the germs produce a nerve-paralysing poison, with resultant stiffness and muscle spasm. It is not commonly reported in dogs, but care should be taken to treat deep wounds according to their form and arrange with the veterinary surgeon to inject with anti-tetanus specific as a safeguard. The patient should be confined to a dark room and put on to a simple menu.

## Minor ailments

ABSCESS

This is a localised collection of pus and matter under a swelling of skin, which has a shiny appearance. With the aid of hot fomentations and gentle pressure it can be made to burst and the pus disposed. Then dress the open wound with 'T.C.P.' or similar preparation dabbed on with a wad of clean cotton wool. When draining the pus away make sure it is done from the lowest point of the abscess when the dog is standing naturally. If normal efforts fail to clear it, it may be necessary to gently pierce the swelling with the point of a sterilised needle; better still, ask the veterinary surgeon to call.

ACCIDENT

If the Boxer has been run over, keep him quiet, treating for shock. Internal injury may be indicated by bloodless gums. Keep the patient warm with blankets, soothing him meanwhile with the voice and hands until the veterinary surgeon arrives.

ACNE

This is inflammation of the skin follicles, causing an eruption of pimples, which eventually break and emit pus, later drying to form scabs. It is usually found on the dog's under-belly and in the area of the stop. It is irritating, and with constant scratching the dog can become distressed. Veterinary advice should be sought, but home treatment entails dusting the acne with medicinal powder after moistening the area with witch-hazel.

ANAL GLANDS

These two small glands are situated one on either side of the anus entrance. In early wild life of the dog they held a foul fluid which the animal would eject at will to make a trail. Domesticity has caused these glands to fall into disuse and they are inclined to clog with waste matter, become chafed and cause distress and discomfort. Signs of this irritation will often be given when the animal rubs his rear along the ground or turns round suddenly to attempt a nibble at his rear parts. The offending matter can be squeezed out simply enough by taking a palm-sized pad of clean cotton wool in the hand, lift up the dog's tail and press the wad hard against the anus, squeezing and kneading the glands. This area should have regular and adequate attention; failure to give attention could easily result in abscesses.

ANAL (AND RECTAL) PROLAPSIS
Common in puppies, occasionally in older dogs. It can be caused by worm infection or straining due to constipation. Whereas the prolapsis can be replaced by the veterinary surgeon under anaesthetic, the *cause* of the straining should be removed without delay.

ANAL TUMOURS
These are usually found in older dogs, arising from small rectal glands. A veterinary surgeon can easily deal with these and there is no reason why they should reappear.

APPETITE, LACK OF
This is usual in worm-infected puppies: it is also a danger signal symptom of the more serious virus infections. The possibility of such infection should be considered if the puppy's temperature is found to be abnormal. In ordinary circumstances, appetite may be improved with a change of diet.

APPETITE, PERVERTED
Puppies and occasionally older dogs, especially bitches have the unpleasant habit of eating coke, stones, even their own and other dogs' stools. The cause is probably some dietetic deficiency and as dogs are natural scavangers, it should not unduly worry the owner. Providing the intake of such things as coal is not excessive, the charcoal additives involved will do good, but it will be as well to revise the animal's diet and step up raw meat feeding with extra vitamins and minerals.

ASTHMA
Fat and overweight dogs usually experience this distressing complaint. The symptoms noted are short, dry coughs, shortage of breath and snuzzly breathing. The first thing to do is get down the animal's weight, give more raw meat in the diet and avoid taxing the heart with heavy exercise.

BAD BREATH
Commonly caused by excess of tartar on and behind the teeth, or ulceration

which has been induced by moisture encrusting in the folds and wrinkles of the face, especially in the case of an elderly dog. When Halitosis is unbearable, action on the teeth and ulceration must be drastic. However, mild cases can be rectified by giving the dog something hard like a marrow bone or biscuit to chew. A weak solution of hydrogen peroxide, applied to the ulceration with a pad of cotton wool will be found effective. The tartar must be scraped away carefully with a special tool available for the purpose.

BALANITIS

A discharge from the male dog's penis, seldom found in a dog at regular stud. A mild solution of antiseptic such as 'T.C.P.' diluted 1:5 in tepid water should be syringed gently beneath the sheath morning and night until the condition is dispersed.

BALDNESS

Often caused by nervous debility, poor condition or glandular thyroid disorder. The diet should be totally revised, ensuring a greater raw meat intake and regular exercise. Synonymous with Alopaecia.

BEE STINGS

Apply 'T.C.P.' or similar antiseptic neat directly to the stings. Give little aspirin to ease pain and treat for shock, as required. If stinging is extensive call the veterinary surgeon.

BILIOUS ATTACK

First signs are usually nausea and vomiting. The dog's temperature should be recorded to ensure that these are not symptoms of something more serious. Be warned by sub-normal or abnormal readings of one degree only and if worried call the veterinary surgeon. Take away solid food and give mixture of white of egg, one teaspoonful of glucose with tablespoonful of boiled water, the whole well beaten. A few drops of brandy can be usefully added. Dosage: One teaspoonful every hour. Keep patient warm and in dark.

BITES

ANIMAL: Antiseptic solution from 'T.C.P.' or Iodine should be dripped into the wound with a pipette or similar dropper, *after* the wound area has been shaved and cleaned. Bad bites should be referred at once to the veterinary surgeon.

SNAKE: The veterinary surgeon should be called at once. First Aid include application or a tourniquet above the bite if it is on foot or leg. Emergency treatment would include cutting a deep 'X' over the bite or fang marks and dripping potassium-permanganate into the wound so made.

BLADDER

INFLAMMATION OF: If the dog can be persuaded to drink large quantities of water or milk it will help to flush out the system and cure the condition, which is one of Cystitis and inclined to persist. The cause can be due to a house-trained dog, habitually clean, forced to hold himself for extended periods. This will result in the bladder becoming distended and inflamed with a rise in body temperature and loss of appetite. Such a condition is for the veterinary surgeon to deal with.

STONES: If a dog's urine, which is acid, is neutralised or becomes alkaline, a sediment is left in the bladder which contributes to the making of small stones, some of which can get lodged in the urethra and cause a blockage. Surgical treatment is necessary, but a consistent raw meat diet helps a lot to prevent such conditions.

WEAKNESS: Usually experienced by older dogs unable to hold themselves for very long, or with the bitch in whelp whose forward puppies are pressing on her bladder, making it impossible for her to be continent. Such animals, being normally clean in their habits, become worried at their lapses. This is where the owner can allay their worries by refraining from scolding and showing understanding. The floor of the sleeping quarters should be lined with newspapers or a sand and dirt box provided. These can be disposed of every morning without fuss and the system kept until the animals have reverted to their normal clean habits or have been re-assured. Sometimes bladder weaknesses indicate kidney disorder, which needs professional veterinary attention.

BLINDNESS

All puppies are born blind, this being Nature's way of protecting them during the first few days of their lives. Until they are nine or ten days old, when they see some daylight, they are unlikely to wander or suffer eye damage. Congenital blindness is quite another matter and rare in the Boxer. It is known as Progressive Retinal Atrophy (P.R.A. for short) and is hereditary. This can be eradicated only through selective breeding.

BOWEL

INFECTION: Enteritis, the most common result of infection, must be treated immediately. It starts off usually with simple diarrhoea which if unattended can deteriorate into a dark, sometimes blood-splattered and unpleasant stool. If allowed to progress further, the animal will become prostrate. The cause must be determined and dealt with as advised by the veterinary surgeon, but initial action is to withdraw all meat feeding and give only milky foods.

BLOCKAGE: Purgatives seldom prove effective in dislodging internal obstructions. Veterinary help must be obtained either to diagnose the trouble, such as a tumour or to remove it by surgery.

BRONCHITIS

A chill might well prove the forerunner of this debilitating complaint. Draughts and failure to rub down a dog after a swim or walk in the rain have been known to cause it. The temperature should be taken; bronchitis usually shows up at between 103 degrees and 104 degrees Farenheit. The patient will need warmth, yet plenty of air movement around him and light feeding such as steamed white fish, gruel and chicken, etc. is indicated. The sometimes severe dry coughing which accompanies this complaint can be alleviated by nasal drops given under veterinary supervision. Some breeders keep a Bronchitis Kennel for such cases. This can be an ordinary box like a tea-chest or travelling box, with a small hole in it through which the spout of a kettle can be directed. A measure of Friar's Balsam or similar can be mixed with the water in the kettle; this should be boiled and the vapour directed through to the dog in the box. Three or four times a day this should be repeated ten minutes at a time until improvement has been noted.

BRUISES

It is seldom possible to see a bruise on a dog without close inspection, his coat hiding a good deal. However, it is obvious that if the animal has been hit by a car, or has cuts and wounds caused by some heavy blow, then bruising exists. Any open wounds or abrasions must be dealt with and bathed with warm water into which a few drops of reliable antiseptic have been poured. Bed with a hot water bottle will do much to relieve local pain and boiled water into which honey has been added makes an advisable feed in the initial stages. Care must be taken with older dogs especially, that the bruising is completely dispersed. If treated casually, permanent stiffness can ensue and aged animals require a lot of reassurance and understanding from their owners at such a time.

BURNS AND SCALDS

Burns produce dry heat injuries, whereas scalds are moist heat effects. The same treatment can be directed to both forms, but first treat for shock and keep the patient quiet, giving him a teaspoonful of bicarbonate of soda followed by as much fluid in the form of warm milk and glucose as he will take. Bicarbonate of soda should also be applied to the affected area in pack form after removing any impeding coat. The mixture should be in the form of 1 oz. to 1 pt. of boiled water, and soaked into a pad which will adequately cover the wound. After effects of burns and scalds are frequently severe. Great care should be taken to ensure that infection is kept at bay and diet should be as nutritive as possible, with ample protein such as raw meat to build up the patient once he is convalescent. Never use oils or ointments for treatment as these are capable of generating heat.

CANKER (OF THE EAR)

The affected dog will invariably show his discomfort by holding his head on one side, shaking it and pawing the affected ear. On inspection, it will be found that the ear channel is clogged with a dark brown waxy substance which is hard and emits a pungent odour, which is most unpleasant. Treatment must be given at once and properly applied the condition will be easily corrected. It is always a bit hazardous to use implements in the ear, so as far as possible remove some of the hard, waxy lumps with the fingers and thumb. If this proves too difficult, small tweezers should be employed, but with the greatest care, and gentleness. Sometimes the ear will be found discharging and this will mean it will have to be dried out with small pieces of cotton wool which are securely wrapped round a wooden cocktail stick from which the point has been severed, but only if it is not possible to succeed with the fingers. A useful remedy is 'Otosporin', two drops of this being inserted down the ear channel twice a day for three days, then massaged well in, but the ear must be dry before this is done, also cleaned out thoroughly. On the fourth day, clean the ear, as usual, and lower a $\frac{1}{4}$-teaspoonful of Boracic powder into the channel. Do this twice a day until the canker has disappeared. If the patient seems disturbed and is in pain, an aspirin should be given just before he retires. It should be part of the regular grooming to check up on the Boxer's ears. In this way, no abnormal condition is allowed to progress to become chronic.

CATARACTS

This is opacity of the lens and can occur in both eyes. It is met occasionally in older Boxers, when vision is seriously impaired. Surgery can be employed with hope of moderate success, but it is a progressive condition and not a great deal seems to be known about it as far as dogs are concerned, probably because serious eye conditions are difficult to treat in animals.

CAT BITES

Cat bites and scratches are dangerous in that they are frequently germ-laden, the bites particularly being deep and inaccessible. The bitten area should be shaved and bathed with 'T.C.P.' and the prudent owner would arrange for his dog to receive an anti-tetanus, or similar injection.

CHOKING

Death can quickly result from any obstruction in a dog's throat. Asphyxiation can be prevented by trying to hook it out with the forefinger, providing it can be reached. If the object lies back too far the best thing is to push it further down. Two people are best to cope with an incident like this; one to force open the dog's jaws, the other to probe for the obstruction. The chances of getting bitten in the process have to be weighed against the dog's life being saved. Many such affairs can be prevented by making sure he does not play with objects like rubber toys, small bones and chunks of wood without supervision. Watch too for oversize and gristly lumps of meat in his food, for these are main perils.

CHOREA: (See: Distemper).

CLEFT PALATE

This is where the hard roof of the dog's mouth is cleft instead of being flat. A congenital fault, it causes the animal to blow out through the nostrils the milk he suckles through the mouth, due to no vacuum being formed in the mouth. Such unfortunate puppies are better painlessly destroyed as surgery is not successful.

COLIC

An advanced form of indigestion which can cause the dog great discomfort. Warmth and local massage will usually put right the matter, but when attacks persist dose the Boxer with one teaspoonful of ordinary bicarbonate of soda.

COLITIS

A painful and often difficult condition to treat. The larger bowel is inflamed and diarrhoea and anaemic effects are noted symptoms. Nursing entails rest, reassurance and light diet.

COLLAPSE

This resembles shock and treatment must be given accordingly. It can be caused following an accident on the road or a fight, or even due to a heart condition. The temperature when taken will be found on the low side and breathing is shallow. Lay the dog on his right side, raise the hindquarters, keeping the head low. If he is *conscious* and seems able to swallow put a few drops of brandy on the back of his tongue. Never give anything orally to an unconscious patient. The veterinary surgeon must be called in such cases.

CONSTIPATION

This is frequently caused by too much starchy food such as biscuit meal in excess of raw meat. etc. However, the cause must first be explored for bowel stoppages must not be discounted if the condition persists. Exercise should be increased with general toning up and the dog's diet must be improved at once. To cope with ordinary constipation there are a number of good proprietary laxatives on the market. Chronic cases should be referred to the veterinary surgeon.

CONCUSSION

Normally brought about by a heavy blow on the head. The dog should be kept warm in a darkened room and a stone hot water bottle put in his bed and covered with an old sock or similar. Call the veterinary surgeon, but first aid can be rendered by applying cold compresses to the head. The dog should not be dosed through the mouth.

CYSTS

These can spring up on the dog's back, in fact on any part of his body, but they appear more commonly as interdigital cysts. They prove painful and the dog is usually rendered lame, for the cysts are like small boils. Dipping the dog's feet into warm water or applying a few poultices will often bring the cysts to bursting point, when they should be bathed with a weak antiseptic solution. Persistent cysts may require surgical treatment, but a *complete* change of diet is recommended before resorting to this, a trial diet of from three to four weeks being best.

CYSTITIS (See: Bladder Infection).

CUTS

The cuts should be bathed over carefully with warm water to assess their severity. If the wound extends beyond one inch, it may require suturing by the veterinary surgeon. The surface of the cut should be protected with lint and bandage meanwhile and the 'lips' of the wound should be compressed together to hasten healing.

DEMODECTIC MANGE

This is sometimes known as 'red' mange, due to the reddening of the affected parts. It causes intense discomfort with some thickening of the tissue. The patient loses appetite and condition and the veterinary surgeon should advise treatment for this is not easily cured.

DERMATITIS

This takes the form of an eczema with red and raw suppurating areas which eventually become encrusted. Surrounding hair should be carefully trimmed away, the affected parts dressed with antiseptic and drying remedies which the veterinary surgeon will prescribe.

DIABETES

The dog quickly loses condition, although his appetite is abnormal and he seems to require a lot of liquid. Urine is light in colour and laboratory tests will reveal excessive sugar content. Tiredness and diarrhoea, with possible vomiting, can be expected. He should be put on to raw meat diet with a small pinch of bicarbonate of soda at every meal. Treatment is a matter for the veterinary surgeon.

DIARRHOEA

This is Nature's way of cleansing the body of impurities and waste matter, absorbed in the form of unsuitable food, etc. However, the condition is represented in the pattern of several virus diseases such as Distemper, etc., and when diarrhoea persists unabated for more than two days, in spite of careful treatment, it needs to be viewed very seriously. The first effort should be to harden up the dog's motions. Raw meat feeding should be withdrawn and he should be put entirely on milky meals – bread and warm milk is particularly good in halting transitory diarrhoea. If some increase in temperature is noted, the veterinary surgeon should be called in immediately to ascertain its cause.

DISCHARGES

These need prompt attention, for quite apart from being unpleasant, some form of infection is implied, and the veterinary surgeon should be asked to investigate at once.

DISCHARGE FROM TEATS: (See: Chapter Three. Nursing Problems/Excess Milk).

DISCHARGE FROM PENIS: (See: Balanitis).

DISCHARGE FROM RECTUM: (See: Anal Glands).

DISCHARGE FROM WOUNDS: If the dog can reach the cut with his tongue, this will prove the best medicine. If he cannot, then the discharge – which is serum oozing from the broken skin – can be dealt with by constant bathing with a weak solution of 'T.C.P.' – allowed as much fresh air as possible and the patient given plenty of exercise.

DISCHARGE FROM VAGINA: This is usually experienced by a bitch after whelping. She will have no appetite and become weaker. It must be checked that she did not retain any afterbirth during her whelping, for this can prove very dangerous and peritonitis can develop, or other septic condition. The veterinary surgeon can inject with Pituitrin to offset this and he should be called in to deal with all abnormal discharges. Occasionally, after a bitch has been mated she will re-commence blood flow from the vagina. This must be examined at once as any disruption of the oestral flow should be viewed with suspicion. Likewise, careful watch should be kept on such a bitch during the gestation of her puppies to ensure normal progress.

DISCHARGE FROM MOUTH: (See: Bad Breath).

DISCHARGE FROM EYES: The commonest form is conjunctivitis, which is a weeping condition. This can be cleared up quickly enough, using a conventional veterinary product, although it is liable to recur mildly at intervals. However, more serious eye troubles than this exist to worry the dog and his owner and such forms as DISTICHIASIS, ECTROPION and ENTROPION are discussed in this Chapter.

DISCHARGE FROM NOSE: A dog perspires through his nose and it is a sign of good health if there is a constant and clear slight discharge to dampen it. However, if mucus is noted from the nostrils the matter needs urgent attention as this could be the beginning of something serious.

DISLOCATIONS

The commonest dislocation experienced is in the hip joint, toe joints being next in order. An X-ray will be required to determine the degree of dislocation and to ensure there is no fracture. The dog should be laid in as near to a natural position as possible and restrained from movement until the arrival of the veterinary surgeon. If the patient seems anxious and restless, a sedative should be given.

DISTICHIASIS

An unpleasant condition of the eye where a double row of lashes grow on the lids and turn slightly inwards. The eyeball is continually brushed and irritated, causing copious weeping. Surgery can be employed to remove the superfluous lashes; home treatment with a pair of eyebrow tweezers providing little more than temporary relief.

DROWNING

Employ artificial respiration after the dog has been laid on his side. The flat of the hand should push down firmly against the ribs, then lifted sharply, the action being repeated at strict intervals of about eighteen exhalations a minute for a Boxer. It should be noted that it is important to keep the dog's tongue extended from the mouth during treatment. An assistant can sometimes be usefully employed doing this while artificial respiration is applied.

DRY ECZEMA

Another form of Mange. The patches are usually grey, rather like elephant skin to touch and these will become pustular but dry over quickly. The dog will be intensely irritated and scratch and cause further encrustment. Veterinary advice should be sought for the cause.

ECLAMPSIA

A condition experienced by bitches while nursing. It is caused by sudden deficiency of calcium in the bloodstream, the normal supply having been used up in milk production for the puppies. Matrons, rather than young mothers are mainly affected, those with especially large litters being most smitten. The first signs of the trouble include some panting and twitching and a stagger when rising, also a distinct change in expression, which seems dazed. When this is noted in a lactating bitch, call in the veterinary surgeon at once. He will probably inject heavily with calcium and the bitch will become normal, although exhausted within half-an-hour. She should be rested away from her litter if possible, and the puppies themselves given supplementary feeds of 'Lactol', according to their size and age.

From this point, the bitch should be under constant supervision. She will need a further injection during the day, although the extra booster feeds allowed the puppies will ease off their absorption of calcium from the dam. The latter should be encouraged away from the youngsters at ever-increasing intervals once she has shown pre-disposition to Eclampsia until at the end of a month she can remain isolated from them for at least an hour. In this 'break' she should be given as much fresh-air exercise as she can take, but care must be taken that she does not become anxious, for worry can bring on an attack of Eclampsia quite effectively. If she picks up a puppy in her mouth and seems to be wandering about aimlessly with it, this could be a sign of an attack and she should be dosed with Collo-Cal-D, according to the producer's instructions forthwith, when she will become serene once more. Once she has completed her natural process as a nursing mother of course, she is unlikely to be further affected.

ECTROPION
This is a condition where the eyelids turn slightly outwards failing to give protection to the eyes from dust, pollen, etc. The haw is visibly exposed. The condition can be remedied by surgery.

ECZEMA
This is a skin condition which starting with bare patches becomes pustular and breaks with a discharge which eventually encrusts, causing severe irritation. The hair around the affected area must be trimmed away and the patches dressed with suitable antibiotic dressing, cortisone for example having been found effective. This form of skin disorder is inclined to develop a weeping spread under the scabbing. The veterinary surgeon must be consulted for up-to-date treatment.

ENCEPHALITIS: (See: Hardpad)

ENTROPION
This is an eye condition where the eyelids turn slightly inwards, usually the lower lids. It is an inherited fault and if not deal with the eye cornea will be damaged. Correction is a surgical matter.

EPISTAXIS
Nose-bleeding, caused either by a blow on the nose or by foreign bodies in the nasal membranes. If the latter it may prove necessary to get veterinary treatment. If the former, the blood flow can be arrested by applying ice-packs.

EPILEPSY
There appears to be no cure for this. The dog will fall to the ground,

twitching, sometimes whimpering. Sedatives can be given and the animal will appear none the worse. Minor fits such as teething convulsions are caused by pain in the gums, but these are a passing phase which can be obviated if the puppy is given a large marrow bone to gnaw and help his teeth come through.

GASTRO-ENTERITIS

Diarrhoea is the usual symptom and in advanced cases it is often marked with blood, at which stage it is serious. Vomiting is noted and this has the appearance of beaten white of egg. Abdominal pain is evident, but not necessarily any rise in temperature. The dog should be taken off meat and put on to milky foods at once. It is better if he is segregated from his companions too. All such bowel disorders should entail veterinary advice.

GLAUCOMA

This causes enlargement of the eyeball brought about by pressure of fluid inside. It is a hereditary condition and serious therefore.

GRASS SEEDS

The summer months, especially that of July find brittle, ripe stalks in the fields. These will split and the little florets from the seed heads will penetrate the dog's skin beneath his coat and between his toes. Lameness and consequent irritation ensues, sometimes small bumps rising on his back. The seeds should be withdrawn and the puncture made swabbed over with antiseptic solution.

HARE-LIP

A congenital deformity, usually associated with Cleft Palate, already discussed. The lip has an open division making it impossible for the puppy to suckle effectively.

HARVESTERS (OR HARVEST MITES)

Small red creatures the colour of red pepper which abound the fields in summer. They cluster on the dog wherever they make contact and cause intense irritation. The best treatment is to dust him with Gammexane powder as soon as he is back home.

HEAT STROKE

Often caused by thoughtless owners leaving their dog in a closed car during hot weather. A dog so mishandled should be limited to a drink of cold water to which a little salt has been added. His body should be bathed gently with cold water.

HERNIA

It is not uncommon for first-born puppies or those bred from a maiden, therefore inexperienced dam, to have a protuberant navel. This is caused by the agitated mother pulling on the umbilical cord, or by a dam whose extreme undershot jaw will disallow a clean bite of the cord close up to the whelp. Small bumps thus produced in the puppy's navel area are of little consequence and few would describe them as being unsound. However, puppies with large bumps are probably best left unpurchased, although veterinary treatment is invariably successful, but expensive.

There are other forms of hernia known as Inguinal Hernia (sometimes noted in a bitch's groin), the Scrotal Hernia and the Diaphragmatic Hernia. The last-named can be caused by an accident. All these are far more serious than the common Umbilical form referred to and need prompt surgical treatment.

HYSTERIA

This mental disturbance, like the ordinary fit, although distressing to watch does not appear to worry the individual unduly, once the phase has passed. Worms, teething pains, etc. have been blamed for Hysteria. It is also engaged with the aftermath of Distemper. When it occurs the dog should be taken at once to a quiet, dark room, taking care to avoid being bitten. He should be left there until the fit has taken its course, making sure of course, that nothing remains in the room with him which could cause him serious injury.

INCONTINENCE (See: Bladder Weakness).

LEANNESS

Some Boxers seem never to furnish enough in body to complete correct balance with substance. A well-used stud dog is often such a problem to his owner, especially if the dog is wanted for exhibition too. The difficulty arises too with young males in the process of sexually adjusting themselves. Although not necessarily true, it is usually found that once the appetite can be promoted the dog will put on weight. Vitamin-E Succinate is a useful encouragement and Wheat Germ Oil capsules will be found helpful. Appetites can be 'tickled' with tasty morsels such as cubes of Cheddar cheese, etc. but it is not suggested that the Boxer should be indulged beyong the realms of commonsense. Vitamin-B can also be used to good effect when a dog needs more weight.

LICE

These tiny grey insects burrow under the dog's skin and cause him considerable irritation because he finds it impossible to dislodge them. The eggs can often be noted clinging to his coat and unless they are promptly removed and disposed of they will hatch out in less than a week and use him as their host. 'Gammexane' powder must be dusted liberally into his coat and a course of baths, using 'Seleen Suspension' will dispose of the lice and their eggs completely. The coat is sponged over thoroughly for at least ten minutes, but not rinsed. The dog should then be dried off.

MANGE

Like skin trouble in humans, the subject is only superficially understood, its forms appearing in such variety. Apart from the Eczemas and ordinary Dermatitis and Ringworm, covered individually in this chapter, the two kinds which concern most are Sarcoptic and Follicular (or Demodectic) Mange.

FOLLICULAR MANGE: This is caused by a mite which burrows into the follicles of the skin, causing the hair to fall out in small quantities at a time. The area so affected will become bare, red and raw and although at first the patches will appear on the cheeks, the skull and foreparts in sections not much larger than a 5p piece, they will eventually merge together substantially. A dog in an advanced state of the disease can be virtually denuded of coat. It will be found that the affected skin areas thicken perceptibly and look as though they have been dusted with a white ash or powder. The mites appear to emit a sort of poison which gradually debilitates the dog and can eventually prove fatal, for the victim becomes not only distressed with the irritation but seems to sink into a state of melancholia. On the other hand, if this pernicious mite is caught early in its attack it can be dispersed. There are a number of good proprietary remedies on the market and extra good feeding and exercise contributes to successful results. It is a disease which seems to attack the short-coated breeds more and care must be taken to ensure that all bedding used by a patient is destroyed and the kennel scrupulously cleaned out with strong disinfectant, for the mite can pass from one dog to another.

SARCOPTIC MANGE: This too is caused by a mite and causes intense irritation. It is usually noticed for the first time by what appears to be acne on the underbelly and inner thighs of the dog. On inspection it is clearly not acne but pustular spots as found in dry eczema, which break and encrust, forming scabs. Some hair loss is experienced and the skin becomes very dry. All kinds of remedies have been used including sulphur baths, polar bear's grease and various 'secret' recipes. Very often such afflictions beset a dog below par in health. As with other manges referred to, it is the first essential to condition the animal with nutritive food and exercise, giving him a sound and healthy internal groundwork for external treatment.

NEPHRITIS

Kidney inflammation, causing considerable pain, is sometimes caused by renal calculi, which are stones in the kidneys. In young dogs Leptospira canicola can infect through contact with the urine of dogs already infected. Loss of appetite, lumbar pains, thirst and vomiting, with coated tongue. A serious condition generally, and one likely never to be entirely dispersed.

NERVOUSNESS

This is a condition most undesirable in the Boxer and viewed askance in any breed, for that matter. It can be due to close in-breeding, haphazard breeding or bad environment and ill-treatment. Sometimes it stems from puppyhood, when a dog is picked up suddenly and cruelly or the dog is left alone and hungry for extended periods. Bitches, for example, are sometimes forbidden the chance of a quiet and easy pregnancy. They should be kept away from annoyances and irritations until well after their puppies have been born. The best treatment for a nervous dog is reassurance by his owner. It can be soon discovered what brings an individual into a condition of fear and until he can face that situation again without a tremor, he should be conditioned, or trained to meet it. A good nerve tonic for dogs is Scullcap, from the plant Scutellaria, otherwise known as Helmet Flower. This forms an excellent herbal remedy.

OBESITY

A fat Boxer is anathema. Quite apart from spoiling his general appearance, the extra weight around the loins militates against the athletic prowess expected of the breed and shortens his life. His food will have to be arranged on a strict diet, cutting out any thing which is liable to fatten and concentrating almost entirely on raw meat. If these measures have no effect, the cause might be glandular, in which case the veterinary surgeon must be asked to diagnose.

POISONS

All cases of poisoning should be referred at once to the veterinary surgeon. First aid must be in the form of an emetic. This can be either a dessertspoonful of common salt in a quarter pint of water or a similar solution of mustard. A marble sized piece of common soda will be effective too. If you know or suspect the cause of poisoning tell the veterinary surgeon when you telephone him. He will then be able to guide you in the treatment of the individual form.

PROGRESSIVE AXONOPATHY (PA)

A disease of the central nervous system found only in Boxers, although somewhat similar hereditary diseases have been noted earlier in breeds such as the Alaskan Malamute and the Boston Terrier. The mode of inheritance in Boxers is by a recessive gene, allied to that for white puppies. The carriers seem to be found within a small number of bloodlines and if a vet in general practice suspects a puppy has PA he should be asked to refer it to one of the named diagnostic centres for definite analysis. Much has been done to combat this neurological disease: a Master Plan has been drawn up by an expert panel formed by the Boxer Breed Council and today its effect has been lessened to a point where the likelihood of any adult Boxer developing PA, whatever its ancestry, is negligible.

RICKETS

This condition has been largely dispersed in dogs today due to the greater interest shown in them and better pre-natal care, and scientific rearing. A sufferer will have enlarged joints, with a tendency to walk almost on the hocks. The spine will be arched and the front bowed. Such a dog will never entirely cast off the condition, even with the best possible feeding and care, but he can be vastly improved upon by concentrating on highly nutritive foods such as raw, fresh beef, fresh eggs, milk and balanced calcium additives as soon as the condition has been diagnosed.

RINGWORM

A skin disease capable of being transferred to humans. The hair becomes thin and detached, making small round patches on the coat in typical ring shape. It is a fungoid disease and needs specialised veterinary treatment.

ROUNDWORM

Many dogs are infested with roundworm, but it is puppies who appear the main sufferers. The worm is easily dispersed these days, there being many proprietory medicines available to dog owners. In appearance the roundworm looks like vermicelli. It is creamy-pink in colour and about 4 in. to 5 in. long. Care has to be taken when dosing very young puppies and it is as well to let the veterinary surgeon arrange this unless the breeder is experienced and knows what he is doing. At one time it was necessary to starve a puppy prior to dosing, but modern methods do not require this. Usually one treatment will suffice, the worms being emitted orally and through the anus in coils. However, some breeders prefer to treat again when the puppies are about eight weeks old, the first attempt being a milder one at say five weeks of age. Once free from roundworm, the youngster will make rapid strides and thrive well.

TAPEWORM

An unpleasant parasite, its small segments adhering to the dog's anal region, revealing the infestation, which usually attacks adults rather than puppies. These segments look rather like grains of rice, but the worm itself can be many feet long inside the dog. It resembles a strip of creamy coloured tape or ribbon and causes great listlessness in its host. The dog's coat will be affected and he is likely to emit a pungent odour from body and breath. The Tapeworm is believed to be contracted either from the flea or by eating rabbit. The veterinary surgeon will know how to expel the worm quickly but treatment should be repeated twice yearly as reinfestation is likely.

# 9 Glossary of Terms

These include the terms usually found in British and American dog show parlance, together with a few which might be encountered in German pedigrees, records and training literature. The latter are indicated thus – (*Germ.*). The Author thanks Mrs Pat Withers for her help in this section.

ABZEICHEN: (*Germ.*) The dog's coat markings.

ADEL: (*Germ.*) Nobility.

AFFIX: A name granted by the Kennel Club General Committee to a breeder allowing him the sole right to use such affix as part of a name when registering or changing the name of a dog. Where the Grantee of a registered Affix wishes to use it when naming a dog bred by him or which was bred from parents which were bred by him, then the Affix must be used as a *prefix* (as the first word of a dog's name). Otherwise it must be used as a SUFFIX (the last word of a dog's name).

AHNENTAFEL: (*Germ.*) Pedigree.

ALTER: (*Germ.*) Age.

ANGULATION: The angles formed where the bones meet at the joints. When applied to the hind limb it refers to the correct angle formed by the true line of the haunch bone, femur and tibia. In the forelegs it would refer to the line of shoulder bone, radius bone and humerus. Lack of angulation suggests straightness in these joints and such a condition could be reasonably considered an unsoundness.

A.O.V.: Any Other Variety. A show term used to indicate that class entries are invited from any other variety than the breed entered for in a previous class.

APPLE HEADED: With the skull rounded on top as in Toy Spaniels. A feature undesirable in the Boxer.

AUGEN: (*Germ.*) Eyes.

AUSBILDUNG: (*Germ.*) Training.

AUSDRUCK: (*Germ.)* Expression.

A.V.: Any Variety. A term used to indicate that entries are invited from any variety of breeds, including those entered from earlier classes. This applies to shows, stake classes and Field Trials.

B. or b: Abbreviation for bitch, as described in dog show catalogues and on show entry forms.

BAD-DOER: A dog who thrives poorly, however well fed and cared for. Often, such a dog has never done well, even from birth.

BAD-SHOWER: A dog who cannot, or will not display himself properly and to advantage at shows. This can be due to boredom, obstinacy or nervousness.

BALANCE: Co-ordination of the muscles giving graceful action coupled with the overall conformation of the dog, the lateral dimensions of the dog should mould pleasingly with his vertical and horizontal dimensions. Equally, the head and tail should conform and contribute pleasingly to the balance of the dog's outline.

BARRELLED: A term pertaining to ribs which are strong and well rounded (like a barrel), allowing plenty of heart room.

BEFEHL: (*Germ.*) Command.

B.B.: Abbreviation for Best of Breed.

BEEFY: Over-development of the hindquarters, which are thus rendered coarse.

BELEGT: (*Germ.*) Mated.

BENCHED: Pertaining to a show where the dogs exhibited are relegated to benches.

BESITZER: (*Germ.*) Owner.

BESITZWECHSEL: (*Germ.*) Change of ownership.

BITCHY: An effeminate male.

BITE: Refers to the position of the upper and lower incisors when the dog's mouth is closed.

BLAZE: A white marking (usually bulbous) running up the centre of the face on some Boxers. Also applied casually to white neck collar markings.

BLINDENFÜHRERHUND: (*Germ.*) Abbreviation = Bl.H. Guide Dog for the Blind.

BLOOM: Glossiness or good sheen of coat, especially desirable on a Boxer.

BLOCKY: Term used to describe the brachycephalic head, such as the Boston Terrier's. Also used to describe a short, stocky, cobby body such as the Bulldog's.

BONE: A well-boned dog is one possessing limbs giving an appearance and feel of strength and spring without being coarse.

BR.: Breeder, i.e. the owner of the dam of the puppies at the time of whelping.

BRACE: Two dogs of the same breed exhibited together.

BRINDLE: A mixture of dark and light hairs giving a generally dark effect, usually being lighter streaks or bars on a grey, tawny, brown or black background.

BRISKET: That part of the body in front of the chest and between the forelegs.

BROKEN COLOUR: Where the main coat colour is broken up by white or other hairs.

BROKEN-UP FACE: A face which shows a combination of lay-back, projecting lower jaw and wrinkle, as seen in such breeds as the Bulldog and Pug.

BROOD BITCH: A female kept solely for breeding purposes.

BRUSTTIEFE: (*Germ.*) Depth of Brisket.

B.S. or B.I.S.: Best in Show or Best in Sex. A dog who has beaten all others or all others in this sex, respectively.

BURR: The irregular formation of the inner ear.

BUTTERFLY NOSE: When the nostrils are mottled and show flesh colour against the black pigment.

CAT FEET: Short, round and 'tight' feet with compact, thick pads, the toes well muscled-up and arched.

C.C.: Challenge Certificate. A Kennel Club award signed by a judge for the best dog of his sex in breed at a Championship Show.

CH: Champion. The holder of three C.Cs. awarded and signed by three different judges.

C.D.: Companion Dog. One holding this degree has passed a test for obedience and reliability.

C.D.(X).: Companion Dog (Excellent). A degree indicating that the holder has passed a severe test for obedience and reliability.

CHARACTER: A combination of the essential points of appearance and disposition contributing to the whole, and distinctive to the particular variety of dog to which the holder belongs.

CHEEKY: Exceptional development of the cheek muscles and cheek tissue.

CHOPS: The pendulous upper lips common to the Bulldog and certain Hounds.

CLODDY: A low and very thick-set build.

CLOSE COUPLED: Short in back and loins.

COBBY: Of compact, neat and muscular formation. Like a cob horse.

CORKY: Compact, nimble in mind and body, lively and spirited.

COUPLING: That part of the body between the last ribs and the hip joints joined by the backbone.

COW-HOCKS: A dog is said to have cow-hocks when his hocks are bent inwards, thus throwing the hind feet outwards. A structural fault.

CREST: The upper part of the dog's neck.

CROPPING: The practice of trimming a dog's ears to make them small and to stand erect according to the requirements of his breed. This is forbidden in Britain and some American states, but common in Europe.

CROSS-BRED: The issue of parents of two different pedigree breeds.

CROUP: The area adjacent to the sacrum and immediately before the root or set-on of the tail.

CRYPTORCHID: The male dog whose testicles are abnormally retained in the abdominal cavity. Ineligible for show ring competition.

CUSHION: The fullness of the foreface obtained by the padding of the upper lips, in such breeds as the bulldog and Mastiff.


D. or d.: The abbreviation for the Dog (Male) as described in dog show catalogues and/or entry forms.

DAM: The female parent of puppies. The term is generally used, but it has special reference to the bitch from the time she whelps the puppies to the time when she has finished weaning them.

DECKEN: (*Germ.*) To cover (as by a stud dog).

DECKTAG: (*Germ.*) Day for the mating.

DEUTSCHES HUNDESTAMMBUCH: (*Germ.*) Official German Stud Book.

DEW-CLAWS: Rudimentary fifth digits and claws found on the insides of the legs below the hocks. These should be removed from Boxer puppies a few days after birth.

DEWLAP: The loose pendulous skin under the throat. This is highly undesirable in the Boxer.

DIENSTHUND: (*Germ.*) Service Dog.

DIENSTSUCHHUND: (*Germ.*) A Police Dog trained for tracking.

DISH-FACED: A concavity in the muzzle of the dog causing the nose to be tilted slightly higher than the stop.

DOCKING: Shortening the dog's tail by amputation.

DOGGE: (*Germ.*) Great Dane.

DOME: Term which refers to the rounded skull in some dogs, such as the Spaniel.

DOWN-FACED: The opposite to dish-faced (q.v.) when the nose-tip is well below the level of the stop due to a downward inclination of the nose.

DOWN IN PASTERNS: Pasterns which being weak and sagging show an angle of the front feet forward and outward instead of the correct pastern (straight in line from the forearm to the ground).

DRITTER: (*Germ.*) Third.

DUDLEY NOSE: Wholly flesh- or coffee-coloured nostrils; quite distinct from the Butterfly Nose.

ELLENBOGEN: (*Germ.*) Elbows.

ELTERN: (*Germ.*) Parents.

ENKEL: (*Germ.*) Grandson.

ENKELIN: (*Germ.*) Granddaughter.

ERSTER: (*Germ.*) First.

FANCIER: One who is interested in some phase of livestock breeding.

FARBE: (*Germ.*) Colour.

FEHLER: (*Germ.*) Faults.

FILLED-UP: Usually refers to a dog's face with bulky cheek muscles and plenty of wrinkle, such as the Bulldog's.

FLANK: The dog's side between the last rib and hip.

FRONT: What can be seen of the front part of the dog except the head, having special reference to the soundness of brisket and forelegs.

FÜHRER: (*Germ.*) Handler.

FLY-EARS: Ears which are semi-erect and stand out from the side of the head.

FLEWS: The pendulous inner corners of the lips of the upper jaw.

GAIT: How a dog walks, trots or runs.

GOOD-DOER: A dog who thrives well without any special treatment. One who has done well from birth.

GEBRAUCHSHUND: (*Germ.*) Working Dog.

GEDECKT: (*Germ.*) Mated.

GELB: (*Germ.*) Fawn.

GESCHLECHT: (*Germ.*) Sex.

GESCHUTZTER ZUCHTNAME: (*Germ.*) Registered Kennel Name.

GESTREIFT: (*Germ.*) Brindled or striped.

GESTROMMT: (*Germ.*) Brindle.

GEWINKELT: (*Germ.*) Angulated.

GEWORFEN: (*Germ.*) Whelped.

GOOSE-RUMP: A sloping croup, falling away too quickly with the tail set-on too low.

GRIZZLE: An iron grey coat colour, sometimes refers to a grey-brindle.

GROSSELTERN: (*Germ.*) Grandparents.

GROSSMUTTER: (*Germ.*) Grandmother.

GROSSVATER: (*Germ.*) Grandfather.

GUN-SHY: One who is frightened at the sight of a gun or its report.

HAAR: (*Germ.*) Coat, Hair.

HALS: (*Germ.*) Neck, throat.

HANDLER: A person who handles the exhibit in the ring at dog shows. More correctly refers to professional handler.

HARE-FEET: Feet which are rather long and narrow, like those of the hare. Undesirable in the Boxer.

HAW: The inner part of the lower eye-lid which is well developed, hanging down as in the Bloodhound. A fault in the Boxer.

HEAT: A bitch is said to be 'on heat' during her oestral period, when in 'season'.

HEIGHT: A dog's height is measured in a perpendicular line from the ground to the top of his shoulders (at the withers).

HINTERLÄUFE: (*Germ.*) Hind legs.

HINTERHAND: (*Germ.*) Hind legs.

HITZE: (*Germ.*) Heat or season.

HOCKS: The joints in the hind legs between the pasterns and the stifles.

HUCKLE BONES: The top of the hip joints.

HÜNDIN: (*Germ.*) Bitch.

HÜNDCHEN: (*Germ.*) Puppy.

HUNDE: (*Germ.*) Dog. Pl. = Hunde. The general term.

IN-BREEDING: The mating of closely-related dogs, done to perpetuate certain desirable characteristics, which exist already, at least to some extent. See Chapter Three (Breeding).

INTERNATIONAL CHAMPION: A dog who has been awarded the title of Champion in more than one country. The term is not recognised officially by The Kennel Club.

INZUCHT: (*Germ.*) In-breeding.

JUNGTIER: (*Germ.*) Puppy.

KAMPIOEN: (*Dutch*) Champion.

KIND: (*Germ.*) Issue or progeny.

KOPF: (*Germ.*) Head.

KOPPEL-KLASSE: (*Germ.*) Brace class.

K.P.H.: (*Germ.*) Dog trained specially for detective police work.

KRIEGSHUND: (*Germ.*) = Kr.H. A dog trained for military service. A war dog.

KRUPPE: (*Germ.*) Croup.

LAYBACK: When the nose of the dog lies well back into the face as in some of the short-faced breeds such as the Bulldog.

LEATHER: The skin of the ear-flap.

LEGGY: So high on the leg that the dog appears unbalanced.

LEVEL MOUTH: When the jaws are so placed that the teeth meet about evenly, neither undershot, nor noticeably overshot.

LINE-BREEDING: The mating of dogs of similar strain, not too closely related. See Chapter Three (Breeding).

LIPPY: When the lips overhang or are developed more than is correct.

LITTER: A family of puppies born to a bitch at one whelping.

LOADING: Refers to over-musculation or heaviness at the shoulders.

LOINS: That part of the body protecting the lower viscera and overlying the lumbar vertebrae between the last ribs and hindquarters. Fatness in the loin area is undesirable in the Boxer.

LONG-COUPLED: The opposite to close-coupled.

LUMBER: A dog having lumber is one with too much flesh, ungainly in appearance and clumsy in action. Not to be confused with the gawkiness of puppies.


MAIDEN: In the widest sense an un-mated bitch, but in exhibition parlance usually a dog or bitch not having won a first prize.

MASK: The dark markings on the muzzle of the Boxer, or the muzzle itself.

MASKE: (*Germ.*) Mask.

MATCH: A form of competition which is usually arranged privately between dog clubs. It is bound by the usual Kennel Club disciplinary rules.

MATRON: A brood bitch. One kept for breeding puppies.

MELDEHUND: (*Germ.*) Army messenger dog.

MELDESCHEIN: (*Germ.*) Registration Certificate.

MONORCHID: A male dog with only one testicle visible and descended into the scrotum. Such dogs are able to sire puppies, but are not considered so reliable as a dog which is entire, i.e. with both testicles descended into the scrotum. They are ineligible for show ring competition and may not be exported unless the defect is made known to the prospective purchaser and accepted by him.

MUZZLE: The projecting part of the head combining the mouth and nose.

N.A.F.: Name Applied For.

N.F.C.: Not For Competition.

NOVICE: In the widest sense an inexperienced breeder or exhibitor, but in exhibition language a dog or bitch not having won two first prizes.

OCCIPUT: The bone at the top of the back of the skull which in some breeds is prominent as in most of the Hound group.

OESTRUM: The menstrual period. Known also as 'on' or 'in heat' or 'in season'. It lasts usually about twenty-one days, the bitch becoming ripe for mating between the tenth and fifteenth.

OUT AT SHOULDERS: Having the shoulders outward in a loose fashion so as structural weakness.

OUT AT SHOULDERS: Having the shoulders outward in aloose fashion so as to artificially increase the width of the dog's front. This is a fault in the Boxer.

OUTCROSS: The mating of unrelated dogs of the same breed but different strain. See Chapter Three (Breeding).

OVERSHOT: Having the upper incisors projecting over and beyond the lower incisors.

PAD: The cushioned sole of the foot.

PARTI-COLOUR: A coat of two or more colours in patches; checkered or harlequin.

PASTERN: The lowest part of the leg below the knee on the foreleg or below the hock on the hindleg.

P.D.: Police Dog. A dog trained for police work.

PIG-JAW: A badly overshot jaw formation.

POLITZEIDIENSTHUND: (Germ.)=Pd.H. A dog trained for police work or retrained by the police for special services.

PREFIX: An obsolete term. See AFFIX.

PRICK EARS: Ears which stand erect.

PUPPY: A dog under twelve months of age.

QUARTERINGS: The junctions of the limbs, referring especially to the hindquarters.

RACY: Slight in construction; rather long bodied giving an impression of speed rather than substance.

RANGY: Rather long in body, but with more substance than a racy dog.

RASSEKENNZEICHEN: (*Germ.*) Standard.

RED: A general term for coat colours which range from fallow to chestnut, although more properly applied to the darker coats.

RESERVE: The fourth place after judging, for which a green prize card is awarded. It can refer to the runner-up in a class or a show.

RIBBED-UP: A compact dog with the ribs well barrelled.

RIPPEN: (*Germ.*) Ribs.

ROACH-BACK: A back which arches upwards along the spine with particular emphasis over the loins, as in the Dandie Dinmont Terrier. A fault in the Boxer.

ROSE EARS: Ears which fold over exposing the inner burr.

ROT: (*Germ.*) Red.

RUDE: (*Germ.*) Male.


S. = SIEGER: (*Germ.*) A Champion, (Male) to be noted in many German pedigrees. Champion Bitch = SIEGERIN.

SCH: (or Sch.H.): (*Germ.*) Schutzhund. A dog trained for defence work.

SCHULTERHÖHE: (*Germ.*) Shoulder height.

SEASON: When a bitch menstruates she is said to be 'in season'. The oestral period.

SECOND MOUTH: A dog is said to have his 'second mouth' when his first, or puppy teeth are replaced by permanent teeth.

SECOND THIGHS: The muscular development of the leg between the stifle and the hock.

SELF-COLOUR: When a dog is one whole colour, some allowance being given for toning.

SEMI-ERECT EARS: Ears which are neither pricked nor falling forward. Such ears have usually the tips falling forward.

SEPTUM: The thin line which is seen to divide the nostrils.

SERVICE: A mating. The term given to the act of copulation when a bitch is served by a stud dog. When a fee has been paid and the service has proved unsuccessful, it is usual for the stud dog owner to allow a 'free service'.

SET-ON: The point where the tail is set on to the hindquarters.

SH: SANITÄTSHUND: (*Germ.*) Dog used for Red Cross work.

SHELLY: Applying to the dog's body only which is narrow and shallow.

SIRE: The male parent of a dog or litter of puppies.

SLOPING SHOULDERS: Shoulders which are well laid back and allow the Boxer his typical stride. Shoulders which are upright, i.e. with an obtuse angle made by scapula and humerus, will produce a proppy untypical gait.

SNIPEY: When the dog's muzzle is weak, too long and narrow.

SPLAY FEET: Feet where the toes are spread wide apart.

SPREAD: Refers to the width of the front between the wide-spread forelegs of a breed such as the Bulldog. It can refer to the exaggerated front of any dog exhibited in an out-at-shoulders stance.

SPRING: Refers to elasticity of rib, i.e. when the ribs are well rounded, sound and elastic.

STANDARD: The official description of the ideal dog of the breed, as drawn up by a body of experts in that breed and used as a guide in judging.

STARING COAT: When a dog is out of condition his coat hair will be dry, unkempt and harsh. It will stand up and out from the skin. This is known as 'staring'.

STERN: The tail, normally restricted to sporting dogs.

STIFLE: The joint in the hind leg joining the first and second thighs and corresponding to the human knee.

STOP: The depression between and in front of the eyes.

STRAIGHT HOCKS: Hocks which are almost vertical, lacking resilience.

STRAIGHT SHOULDERS: Shoulders where the scapula and humerus join, forming an obtuse angle, being in almost a straight line and rendering the dog a poor mover.

SUFFIX: A suffix is the name of a kennel which is attached to the end of a dog's name in order to identify him with a particular kennel or breeder. Not to be confused with a prefix which is put before a dog's name. (See AFFIX).

SWAY BACK: A back which dips behind the shoulders because of poor local muscular development.

T.A.F.: Transfer Applied For.

THROATY: When the skin of the throat is too loose.

TICKED: When small marks of another colour appears on the main body colour. Applies usually to small dark black or brown marks on a white ground.

TIE: The term is used to describe the locking union of a mating pair.

TIGER BRINDLE: A mixture of light and dark hairs and stripes on a brindled or mottled ground.

TIMBER: A name for good bonal construction, especially used when referring to the forelegs.

TRACE: A dark, often diffused line running down the spine of some short-coated breeds. More evident during puppyhood it opens out and usually indicates colour richness with maturity.

TRANSFER: A change of ownership of a registered dog, duly reported, paid for and recorded.

TUCKED-UP: When the loins are lifted up as in the Whippet. When seen in a breed such as the Boxer, might indicate stomach pains, and should be investigated.

TULIP EARS: Ears which are carried erect, but curled to nearly resemble a tulip bloom. An old type of ear once common in the Old English Bulldog.

TURN-UP: The underjaw which turns up and out as in the Bulldog.

TYPE: The quality essential to a dog if he is to represent or approximate the ideal model of his breed based upon his breed Standard. (See Chapter Two: The Boxer Standard.)

UNBEKANNT: (*Germ.*) Unknown.

UNDERSHOT: Having the lower incisors projecting beyond the upper, as in the Boxer and Bulldog.

UNSOUND: See Chapter Two (The Boxer Standard).

UNTERSCHRIFT: (*Germ.*) Signature.

UPSWEEP: Synonymous with Turn up.

URGROSSELTERN: (*Germ.*) Great-grandparents.

URGROSSENKEL: (*Germ.*) Great-great-grandson.

URGROSSENKELIN: (*Germ.*) Great-great-granddaughter.

URGROSSMUTTER: (*Germ.*) Great-granddam.

URGROSSVATER: (*Germ.*) Great-grandsire.

VATER: (*Germ.*) Sire.

VENT: Generally indicating the area surrounding the anus.

V.H.C.: Very Highly Commended. A show award fifth in order of placing. It carries no prize money.

VORBEISSER: (*Germ.*) Undershot.

WEEDY: Very lightly constructed, lacking substance.

WEISS: (*Germ.*) White.

WELL-SPRUNG: Well-formed in chest development and spring of rib.

WHEEL-BACK: An arched or convex back; as Roach Back.

WHELPS: Newly born puppies.

WITHERS: The point where the neck joins the body in the region of the shoulders.

W.S. = WELTSIEGER: (*Germ.*) A world champion Dog.
Bitch = WELTSIEGERIN.

WRINKLE: Loosely folded skin, to be noted between the Boxer's ears when he is alerted and to be seen from the root of the nose running downwards on both sides of the muzzle.

ZWEITER: (*Germ.*) Second.

Z. ZWERG: (*Germ.*) The initial which appears in many German pedigrees to identify a Miniature dog.

ZUCHTPRÜFUNG: (*Germ.*) A Breeding Trial Certificate Test.

# Appendix 1

## Breed Clubs and their Secretaries

ANGLIAN BOXER CLUB: Mr R. B. Harker, 31 Mountbatten Avenue, Stamford, Lincs. (Tel. 0780 53069)

BRITISH BOXER CLUB: Mrs P. Knight, Mill House Farm, Mill Street, Harlow Common, Essex. (Tel. 0279 22960)

COTSWOLD BOXER CLUB: Mrs W. Davies, Winnuwuk, Downton Road, Stonehouse, Glos. (Tel. 045 382 2253)

ESSEX AND EASTERN COUNTIES BOXER CLUB: Mrs N. Sasse, Bluebell Lodge, Rayleigh Downs Road, Rayleigh, Essex. (Tel. 0702 524049)

IRISH BOXER CLUB: Mrs V. Rutledge, 43 Tern Crescent, Carrickfergus, Co. Antrim, N. Ireland. (Tel. 08494 66806)

LONDON AND HOME COUNTIES BOXER CLUB: Mrs D. Spencer, 17 Strauss Road, Bedford Park, London W4 1DL. (Tel. 01–995 1893)

MANCUNIAN BOXER CLUB: Mrs D. S. Hall, 251 Ainsworth Road, Bury, Lancs. (Tel. 061–764 5593)

MERSEYSIDE BOXER CLUB: Mrs A. Unsworth, 344 Wigan Road, Atherton, Nr. Manchester. (Tel. 0942 873709)

MIDLAND BOXER CLUB: Mrs M. Buck, 8 Dugarde Place, Barford, Warwickshire. (Tel. 0926 24660)

NORTHERN BOXER CLUB: Mr G. Blake, 57 Arklow Road, Intake, Doncaster, Yorkshire DN2 5LB. (Tel. 0302 68215)

SCOTTISH BOXER CLUB: Mrs D. Mackin, Southcliff, Dunure, Ayrshire, Scotland. (Tel. 029 250 254)

SOUTH WALES BOXER CLUB: Mrs I. Moorman, River Bridge, Langynidr, Crickhowell, Powys NP8 1NA. (Tel. 0874 730313)

SOUTH-WESTERN BOXER CLUB: Mrs B. Murray, Lavender House, Kington Magna, Nr. Gillingham, Dorset. (Tel. 074 785 420)

TRENT BOXER CLUB: Mrs J. Alton, 75 Victoria Road, Selston, Notts. (Tel. 0773 810630)

TYNE, WEAR AND TEES BOXER CLUB: Mr D. Edwards, Kvarner, Broomhill, Houghton-le-Spring, Tyne and Wear DH5 9PT. (Tel. 0783 263709)

# Appendix 2

## A Selected Bibliography

BARBARESI, SARAH M.: *Raise and Train Boxers*, New Jersey, 1982
BREARLEY and NICHOLAS: *The Book of the Boxer*, New Jersey, 1983.
DENLINGER, Milo, G.: *The Complete Boxer*, Virginia, 1958.
DUNKELS, Joan: *The Boxer Handbook*, London, 1951.
GORDON, Dan: *The Boxer*, Chicago, 1947.
KNAPEN, L. P.: *Boxer Betrouwbaar Bewaker*, Blaricum, 1936.
MENZEL, R. and R.: *Uber die Abrichtung des Boxers*, Vienna, *c.*1930. *Uber die Grosse des Boxers*, Bruenn, 1930. *Erkentnisse aus dem Gebiete der Boxerleistungszucht*, Planegg-bei-Muenchen, 1932. *Kurze Bemerkungen zu dem Artikel 'Der Boxer'*, Planegg-bei-Muenchen, 1932.
MEYER, Enno: *Judging the Boxer*, New York, 1945.
NEUMANN, Dr: *Der Boxer*, Muenchem, 1908.
NICHOLAS, Annak: *The Boxer*, New Jersey, 1985.
PISANO, B.: *Boxers*, New Jersey, 1979.
RICCI – :*Die Beurteilung des Boxers*, Berlin, 1926.
ROYLE, J: *The Boxer*, Leicester, 1977.
SCHMOGER, A.: *Der Boxer*, Berlin, 1926.
SOMERFIELD, Mrs E.: *The Boxer*, London, 1968.
STOCKMAN, F.: *My Life with Boxers*, London, 1968.
STOCKMANN, P.: *Der Boxer,* Muenchen, 1926.
VOLPE: *This is the Boxer,* New York, n.d.
WAGNER, J. P.: *The Boxer,* New York, 1946.
WHITE, K.: *The Boxer*, 1985.
WILSON WILEY: *Boxers*, London, 1959.
ZIEGLER, H. E.: *Der Hund Seppl,* 1920.
also:
*Der Boxer :* Unsere Hunderassen No. 8 Stuttgart, 1914–1915.
*Der Boxer :* ex Boxerklub, Planegg-bei-Muenchen, *c.*1932.
*Le Boxer :* ex Boxer-Club de France, Strasbourg, 1930.
*Deutsches Boxer Stammbuch :* (Bd.1.). Muenchen, 1904.

# Appendix 3

## Registrations

From the early years of Boxer registrations in Britain, there has been a steady rise in the figures recorded at The Kennel Club. The war years of 1940–41 showed an inevitable drop of course, but this was common to all breeds. 1956 was clearly the best year, with 7,570 actual registrations, since when the figures have more or less dropped, to 3,727 in 1971, with an encouraging uplift in 1974, although 1977 was a bad year with a mere 971 registrations. The annual figures taken from January to December in each year are as follows:

| | | | | |
|---|---|---|---|---|
| 1933 ... 2 | 1944 ... 246 | 1955 ... 6786 | 1966 ... 4104 | 1977 ... 971 |
| 1934 ... 1 | 1945 ... 399 | 1956 ... 7570 | 1967 ... 4421 | 1978 ... 2669 |
| 1935 ... 14 | 1946 ... 707 | 1957 ... 7020 | 1968 ... 4374 | 1979 ... 3933 |
| 1936 ... 11 | 1947 ... 1412 | 1958 ... 6979 | 1969 ... 4457 | 1980 ... 4430 |
| 1937 ... 48 | 1948 ... 1922 | 1959 ... 7410 | 1970 ... 4230 | 1981 ... 3947 |
| 1938 ... 83 | 1949 ... 2644 | 1960 ... 7137 | 1971 ... 3727 | 1982 ... 4077 |
| 1939 ... 74 | 1950 ... 3647 | 1961 ... 6902 | 1972 ... 3984 | 1983 ... 4693 |
| 1940 ... 33 | 1951 ... 4464 | 1962 ... 6803 | 1973 ... 4039 | 1984 ... 4759 |
| 1941 ... 23 | 1952 ... 4479 | 1963 ... 6029 | 1974 ... 4162 | 1985 ... 5321 |
| 1942 ... 79 | 1953 ... 5592 | 1964 ... 5419 | 1975 ... 3527 | 1986 ... 2395 |
| 1943 ... 139 | 1954 ... 6054 | 1965 ... 5152 | 1976 ... 1422 | (up to 30 June) |

## The Kennel Club

The Kennel Club is the ruling body in dogs in Great Britain. Its patron is Her Majesty the Queen and HRH Prince Michael of Kent FIMI is the President. It has offices at 1 Clarges Street, London W1Y 8AB (General Enquiries 01–493 6651. Registration Enquiries 01–493 2001).

The Objects of the Club are mainly for the purpose of promoting the improvement of dogs, Dog Shows, Field Trials, Working Trials and Obedience Tests and include the classification of breeds, the registration of pedigrees, transfers, etc., the licensing of shows, the framing and enforcement of Kennel Club Rules, the awarding of Challenge Certificates, Champion and other Certificates, the Registration of Associations, Clubs and Societies and the publication of an annual Stud Book and a monthly Kennel Gazette.

These are detailed as follows and their reproduction granted by kind permission of The Kennel Club:

Litter Recording and Registration by the Breeder:
    £5.00 per Litter plus
    £5.00 for each Registered (Named) Puppy and
    £1.00 for each Unregistered (Unnamed) Puppy

| | |
|---|---|
| Registration in Obedience Record (Buff Form 1A) | £5.00 |
| Re-registration | £5.00 |
| Transfer to new Owner | £5.00 |
| Loan or Use of Bitch | £5.00 |
| Change of Name (Affix Holders only) (Pink Form 8) | £5.00 |
| Pedigrees (3-generations) | £3.00 |
| Pedigrees (Export) | £20.00 |
| Registration of Affix | £35.00 |
| Affix Maintenance Fee (Annual) | £10.00 |
| Assumed Name (Exhibitor) | £5.00 |
| Registration of Title | £50.00 |
| Maintenance of Title | £15.00 |
| Registration of Title (Branch) | £10.00 |
| Maintenance of Title (Branch) | £6.00 |

For Shows held under Kennel Club Rules:

| | |
|---|---|
| General Championship Show – offering more than 20 sets of Challenge Certificates with or without Obedience Championship, Licence | £500.00 |
| General Championship Show offering 20 sets of Challenge Certificates or less with or without Obedience Championship, Licence | £125.00 |
| Group Championship Show, Licence | £125.00 |
| Breed Championship Show, Licence | £30.00 |
| Open Show, Licence | £20.00 |
| Limited or Sanction Show, Licence | £5.00 |
| Exemption Show, Licence | £5.00 |
| For permission to hold Matches under Kennel Club Regs. | £5.00 |
| For permission to hold a Championship Obedience Show as a Separate Event or part of a Licence Show | £30.00 |
| For permission to hold an Open Obedience Show as a Separate Event or part of a Licence Show | £20.00 |
| For permission to hold a Limited or Sanction Obedience as a Separate Event or part of a Licence or Sanction Show | £5.00 |

Every Boxer breeder should make a point of registering his puppies at The Kennel Club and encourage others to do the same. Only by increasing the numerical strength of the breed, year by year on the registry can we expect to receive better show classifications, and greater acknowledgement from show promoters; even an increase in the number of Challenge Certificates offered.

The Fees are as revised 1 January 1986 and include VAT.

# Index